THE BEST
Pet Name Book

THIRD EDITION

Wayne Bryant Eldridge, DVM
Illustrations by Tom Kerr

EVER!

ANTONY & CLEOPATRA

BARRON'S

Excerpts from *Old Possum's Book of Practical Cats* by T. S. Eliot, copyright 1939 by T. S. Eliot and renewed 1967 by Esme Valerie Eliot, reprinted by permission of Harcourt Brace Jovanovich, Inc. and Faber and Faber Limited.

Excerpts from "How to Name a Dog" copyright © 1948 James Thurber. Copyright © 1975 Helen Thurber and Rosemary A. Thurber. From *The Beast in Me and Other Animals*, published by Harcourt Brace Jovanovich, Inc.

Excerpts adapted from *The Animals' Who's Who* by Ruthven Tremain. Reprinted with permission of Charles Scribner's Sons, an imprint of Macmillan Publishing Company, and Routledge & Kegan Paul Limited. Copyright © 1982 by Ruthven Tremain.

Peanuts cartoon by Charles Schultz, copyright United Features Syndicate. Reprinted with permission of U.S.F. Inc.

Excerpt from *The Will Rogers Book* by Paula Love, copyright 1972 by Texian Publishing Company. Reprint with permission.

About the Author

Dr. Wayne Bryant Eldridge is a veterinarian, as well as founder of Eldridge Animal Hospital, Pets First Veterinary Center, The Pet Place Veterinary Center and Access Veterinary Care in San Antonio, Texas, where he has practiced his profession for over 30 years.

He earned his undergraduate degree and a Doctor of Veterinary Medicine from Texas A&M University in 1971.

Dr. Eldridge is an author and speaker on various topics pertaining to veterinary medicine and pets. His areas of special interest include animal behavior and the human-animal bond.

All inquiries should be addressed to:
Barron's Educational Series, Inc.
250 Wireless Boulevard
Hauppauge, New York 11788
www.barronseduc.com

International Standard Book No. 0-7641-2499-4

Library of Congress Catalog Card No. 2003045394

Library of Congress Cataloging-in-Publication Data
Eldridge, Wayne Bryant.
    The best pet name book ever! / Wayne Bryant Eldridge ;
    illustrations by Tom Kerr.—3rd ed.
        p.   cm.
    ISBN 0-7641-2499-4 (alk. paper)
    1. Pets—Names.   I. Kerr, Tom.   II. Title.

SF411.3.E43 2003
929.9′7—dc21   2003045394

PRINTED IN THE UNITED STATES OF AMERICA

9 8 7 6 5 4 3 2 1

ACKNOWLEDGMENTS

My parents, Adelene and Jack Eldridge, are to be commended for their unconditional love, for their guidance throughout the years, and for providing me with the means for my education.

I am very grateful to my children, Lori Eldridge and Wayne Bryant Eldridge, Jr. for their faith in me and for their assistance with this book.

Also, Bob O'Sullivan and the staff at Barron's are to be commended for their work to make this book a reality.

DEDICATION

This book is dedicated to all caring pet owners and to the celebration of the human-animal bond.

CONTENTS

And out of the ground the Lord God
formed every beast of the field,
and every fowl of the air;
and brought them unto Adam
to see what he would call them: and
whatsoever Adam called every living creature,
that was the name thereof.

And Adam gave names to all cattle,
and to the fowl of the air,
and to every beast of the fields.

GENESIS 2: *19–20*

INTRODUCTION

During my thirty years as a practicing veterinarian, many of the pets brought to me for their first examinations have had no names—not because of apathy on the owner's part but because of the lack of a guide in the name selection process; thus, the owners of these pets sometimes ask for my suggestions. The thousands of requests that I have received originally prompted me to compile a list of unusual pet names; later, I categorized the growing list according to general subject areas, such as historical names and names of foods. This method of categorization has helped hundreds of my clients choose names—not just any name, but a unique one—for their pets. Consequently, I have decided to organize my categories into a book so that I can assist a wider range of pet owners.

The Best Pet Name Book Ever is a creative guide for naming those special animals in our lives. Some of the names in this book are actual names of my patients taken from the files of my animal hospital; others come from interviews with pet owners; and the remainder results from research into the various categories into which I have classified the names. This book seeks to give you an overview of examples of pet names (in particular, those for dogs and cats, but not exclusively), and by no means constitutes a complete list, because as I've learned, the possibilities are limitless. You should use *The Best Pet Name Book Ever*, then, not as the comprehensive source on this subject, but rather as a tool to spark your imagination.

When choosing one of the names from this book or one of your own invention, you should keep in mind a couple of helpful hints. First, pick a name that your pet can easily recognize. Cats and dogs respond better to one and two syllable words: "Ezekiel" is a creative choice; however, your cat will respond more readily to the shortened "Ziggy" or "Zeke." Also, avoid giving your dog a name that sounds like one of the basic commands ("No," "Down," "Sit," "Stay," "Come," etc.). A dog named "Star" may have difficulty distinguishing her name from "Stay." Nevertheless, do not let these considerations restrict your creativity. If you are determined to name your cat "Dante Alighieri," do so, but plan on calling him "Dan" or "Ali." You can still tell your friends about the famous person for whom the cat is named.

Note: If another name within the same chapter appears in the body of an entry, SMALL CAPITALS make reference to that name—for example:

Cyprus   The island where APHRODITE was born.

"Pretty Boy"

CHAPTER 1

Appearance

What's in a name? That which we call a rose
By any other name would smell as sweet.

William Shakespeare
from *Romeo and Juliet*

The most obvious and simple way to name your pet is by its appearance. This basis for choosing a name works especially well for a new pet whose personality and peculiarities have not yet revealed themselves to you. However, keep in mind that as a pet ages, its appearance may change and the name you originally chose for your animal may no longer apply. For example, "Fur Ball" is a cute name for a kitten, but it may not suit a fully grown tomcat. Still, such a situation where the name may become inappropriate rarely occurs, and basing a pet's name on its appearance can result in a fascinating and appropriate name.

Appearance

Adobe
Agate
Albino
Amber
Ashes
Baby Bear
Baby Boy
Baby Doll
Baby Girl
Baby Kitty
Badger
Bandit
Bat Cat
Bear
Beige-ing
Big 'n
Big Boy
Big Foot
Big One
Big Paw
Big Red
Biscuit
Bits
Bitsie
Bitsy
Black

Black Ace
Black Cat
Black Jack
Blackberry
Blackie
Blacky
Blanca
Blanco
Blanquita
Blinker
Blondie
Blue
Bob Cat
Boots
Bootsie
Boxcar
Brandy
Bright Eyes
Brillo
Britches
Brown Spots
Brownie
Browny
Bruiser
Buffey
Buffie

Buffy
Bunny
Bushy
Butter Fingers
Button
Buttons
Cali
Calico
Calley
Camo (Camouflage)
Caracal
Carbon
Carmel
Caspar
Chalk Paw
Charcoal
Charmin
Checkers
Chiquita
Chocolate
Chops
Chubbs
Chubby
Cinder
Cinnamon
Clay

Cobalt
Coco
Coco Bear
Cocoa
Cookie
Copper
Cotton
Cottonball
Cottontail
Coyote
Crackers
Cream
Crimson
Crystal
Cue Ball
Curlie
Curly
Curry
Cutie
Daffy
Daylight
Diamond
Dinky
Dog
Doll
Domino

Droopy	Fawn	Frosty	Gray Bear
Dust Mop	Feather(s)	Fudge	Gray Cat
Dusty	Flame	Funny Face	Gray Spots
Ebony	Flaps	Fuzz Ball	Hairy
Eclipse	Floppy	Fuzzy	Half Pint
Eight Ball	Flopsy	Genius	Hershey
Ember	Fluffy	Ghost	Hi-Ho Silver
Fancy	Four Paws	Ginger	Hobbles
Fang	Foxie	Ginger Snap	Hog
Fat Boy	Foxy Lady	Gold Cat	Honey
Fat Cat	Freckles	Goldie	Hot Dog
Fatso	Frostie	Gray	Hulk

"Floppy"

Appearance

Husky

Inky

Iota

Ivory

Jaguar

Jaguarundi

Jumbo

Kaffir

Kong

Lefty

Leo

Licorice

Lilly White

Limpy

Lion

Little

Little One

Lobo

Locket

Longfellow
   (a dachshund)

Lumpy

Lynx

Mama Cat

Mama Kitty

Manly

Manx

Many Paws

Mauve

Midget

Midnight

Minnie Paws

Miss Pretty

Mitten(s)

Momma Cat

Momma Dog

Moose

Mother Cat

Mouse

Mud

Muffin

Munchkin

Nugget

Nutmeg

Ocelot

Onyx

Orange Kitty

Oreo

Oso

Panda

Panther

Patches

Paws

Pee Wee

Pepper

Perky

Phantom

Pig

Piglet

Pink Kitty

Pinky

Porker

Porky

Powder

Pretty Boy

Pretty Girl

Pudgy

Puff

Puff Ball

Puffy

Pug

Puma

Pumpkin

Pygmy

Quad Pod

Q Ball

Rags

Rainbow

Raven

Red

Runt

Rusty

Sable

Sage

Sandy

Satin

Sausage Dog

Scottie

Scrawny

Scruffy

Seis (Six-toed cat)

Serval

Shadow

Sherman (tank)

Shinola

Shorty

Sienna

Silky

Slick (a snake)

Slim

Slinky

Smidgen

Smokey

Smudge

Sneakers	Spotty	Ten	Twinkles
Snow	Squat	Tiger	Ugly (Ug)
Snow Bear	Squint	Tiny	Velcro
Snowball	Squirt	Tip	Velvet
Snowflake	Stash (moustache)	Tippy	Weenie Dog
Snowman	Stretch	Tiptoe	Weiner Dog
Snowshoes	Stripe(s)	Tomcat	Whale
Snowy	Striper	Toothpick	Whiskers
Socks	Stripie	Toy	Whitey
Spade	Swirl	Tramp	Whitie
Sparkle(s)	Tabby	Trinket	Wildcat
Speckles	Tar Baby	Tubs	Wolf
Splotch	Target	Tux	Yellow
Spot(s)	Tawny	Twiggy	

"I think it all started when they decided to call me Happy Cat."

CHAPTER 2
Personality

Animals are such agreeable friends—they ask no questions, they pass no criticisms.

George Eliot (Mary Ann Evans)
from *Mr. Gilfil's Love Story*

Personality, like appearance, is one of the most obvious characteristics upon which to base a pet's name. However, as I mentioned in Chapter 1, a new pet's personality may not fully emerge at first and may change as a pet grows older. While it is important to remember these considerations when choosing your pet's name, a name derived from a dominant personality trait will usually prove appropriate throughout your pet's life.

Personality

Amble
Angel
Anxious
Apathy
Attack
Baby Bear
Baby Kitty
Back Talk
Bad Cat
Badger
Ballerina
Bandit
Banshee
Barky
Bear
Blinky
Blitz
Blue
Bomber
Bonkers
Browser
Bully
Candy
Caracal
Chainsaw
Chance

Chancy
Chaos
Charmer
Chase
Chatterbox
Chewie
Chewy
Chuckles
Comet
Cool
Couch Potato
Country
Coyote
Cozy
Crash
Crazy
Crunch
Cuddles
Cujo
Cutter
Daffy
Dancer
Dandy
Dash
Demon
Dennis the Menace

Digger
Ding-a-ling
Dingbat
Dingy
Dirtball
Dodger
Dr. Jekyll
Dracula
Duster
Fearless
Feisty
Fighter
Finesse
Finicky
Flake
Flakey
Flash
Flip
Flounder
Fox
Foxy
Fraidy Cat
Freaky
Freeloader
Friendly
Friskie

Frisky
Front Porch Cat
Fruity
Fury
Gabby
Genius
Ginger Snapper
Goofus
Goofy
Goony
Grabber
Gremlin
Groovy
Grumpy
Gunner
Gypsy
Ham
Happy
Happy Cat
Hiccup
Highball
Hobo
Hokey
Honey
Hoover
Hot Dog

Howler	Looney	Mr. Hyde	Rambler
Hugger	Lover	Nibbler	Ranger
Hunter	Lover Boy	Nibbles	Rascal
Ice	Lover Girl	Nightmare	Rebel
Impulse	Lovey	Noble	Roque
Itchy	Lucky	Nocturne	Rough
Jaguar	Lynx	Nosey	Rover
Jaguarundi	Magic	Ocelot	Rowdy
Jaws	Mama Trouble	Oddball	Ruckus
Jet	Manly	Ornery	Rumble
Jinx	Mate	Pampas	Runner
Joe Cool	Meathead	Peepers	Sassy
Jumper	Meow	Peppy	Saucy
Kaffir	Mew	Pistol	Scamp
Killer	Mew-Mew	Play Kitty	Scarlet
Kinky	Mickey Mouth	Pliers	Schitzo
Kissy	Mischief	Pokey	Scooter
Lady	Miss Piggy	Pompous	Scout
Lefty	Miss Priss	Prancer	Scrapper
Leo	Miss Sassy	Prissy	Scrappy
Licker	Monkey	Puddles	Scratches
Licky	Moody	Puma	Screwball
Lightnin'	Mop	Punch	Serval
Lion	Motor	Pushy	Shadow
Loner	Mouser	Quick	Shady
Lonesome	Moxy	Radar	Sharp

Personality

Shock
Shocker
Shredder
Sir Lick-a-Lot
Sissy
Skamp
Skamper
Skidatel
Sleazy
Sleek
Sleepy
Slipper
Slow Poke
Slumber
Sly
Smooch
Snapback
Snapper
Snappy
Sneaky
Sneezy

Sniffer
Sniffles
Sniffy
Snoopy
Snooze
Snoozer
Snuggler
Snuggles
Solo
Spacey
Speedy
Spinner
Spirit
Splash
Spooky
Spunky
Squeaky
Squiggles
Sticker
Stinky
Stray

Stray Cat
Swishie
Taffy
Tag
Teaser
Teddy Bear
Terminator
Thumper
Tiger
Tom
Tough Cat
Tracker
Tramp
Trip
Tripper
Trooper
Trotter
Troubles
Trusty
Tuffy
Tugger

Turbo
Useless
Vagrant
Valiant
Vampire
Vanity
Wags
Warrior
Watchcat
Watchdog
Weasel
Weedeater
Wicked
Wiggles
Wild Thing
Wildcat
Winker
Winky
Woofer
Worm
Worthless

"Jacques" (and friend)

CHAPTER 3

Human Names

The Naming of Cats is a difficult matter,
. . . First of all, there's the name that the family uses daily,
Such as Victor or Jonathan, George or Bill Bailey—
All of them sensible everyday names.
There are fancier names if you think they sound sweeter,
Some for the gentlemen, some for the dames:
Such as Plato, Admetus, Electra, Demeter . . .

T. S. Eliot
from *Old Possum's Book of Practical Cats*

A pet with a human name tends to have a special relationship with its owner, who often regards the pet as a surrogate child or best friend. In fact, many owners name their pets after a person they have known, a relative, or someone they admire. Frequently, a human name can best depict the character, or nature, of a pet; for instance, "Reginald" vividly suggests the qualities of a basset hound. Likewise, a pet may resemble—hopefully not to a great extent—someone you know. If you can name your pet after this person without offending him or her, then you have further established your pet's unique identity.

Human Names

Aaron	Amelia	Barney	Bobbi
Abby	Amos	Barnie	Bobby
Abe	Amy	Barry	Bonnie
Abigail	Andre	Bart	Boris
Adam	Andrea	Bartholomew	Bosley
Adelene	Andy	Basil	Brad
Adolph	Angela	Bea	Bradley
Adriana	Ann	Beau	Brady
Agatha	Anna	Becky	Brando
Agnes	Anne	Belle	Brandon
Al	Annette	Ben	Brandy
Alan	Annie	Benji	Brent
Albert	April	Bentley	Brett
Alec	Arby	Bernard	Brewster
Alex	Armstrong	Bernie	Brian
Alexander	Arnie	Bert	Bridget
Alfred	Arnold	Bertha	Bridgette
Alice	Arthur	Bessie	Britt
Alisa	Ashleigh	Beth	Brittany
Alison	Ashley	Betsy	Brooke
Allan	Audrey	Bianca	Brooks
Allen	Babette	Bill	Bruce
Allie	Bailey	Billie	Bruno
Allison	Barbie	Billy	Brutus
Amanda	Barkley	Billy Bob	Bryan
Amando	Barnaby	Blaire	Bryant

Bubba	Cecil	Clem	Danielle
Bubba Smith	Celia	Clementine	Danny
Buck	Charles	Cleo	Daphne
Bud	Charley	Cliff	Darcy
Buddy	Charlie	Clifford	Darren
Burt	Charlotte	Clint	David
Buford	Chaz	Clinton	Davy
Butch	Chelsea	Cody	Dawn
Byron	Cher	Colby	Debbie
Calvin	Cheryl	Colette	Dee
Cammie	Chester	Colleen	Dennis
Cammy	Chet	Colline	Derek
Candice	Chris	Connie	Derrick
Carley	Christina	Corey	Devan
Carlos	Christopher	Courtney	Dexter
Carmella	Chuck	Craig	Diana
Carmen	Chuckie	Crystal	Dodie
Carol	Ciel	Curt	Dody
Casey	Cindy	Curtis	Dollie
Casper	Clancy	Cynthia	Dolly
Cassidy	Clancey	Daisy	Dominic
Cassie	Clara	Dale	Dominique
Caterina	Clare	Damon	Don
Catherine	Clark	Dan	Donald
Cathy	Claudia	Dana	Donna
Catrina	Clay	Daniella	Donnie

Human Names

Dory
Dot
Dottie
Doug
Douglas
Drew
Dudley
Duncan
Dustin
Dwayne
Dylan
Earl
Edgar
Edie
Edward
Edwin
Edy
Elaine
Eli
Elisabeth
Elizabeth
Ellen
Ellie
Elliot
Elmer
Elsa

Elsie
Elvira
Emilio
Emily
Emma
Eric
Erik
Erin
Ernest
Ethan
Eunice
Eva
Evan
Evette
Ezra
Faith
Fannie
Fay
Felicia
Felix
Fergie
Fletch
Flo
Floyd
Foster
Fran

Francine
Francis
Frank
Frankie
Frannie
Fred
Freddie
Freddy
Frederick
Gabby
Gary
Gayle
Gene
George
Georgette
Georgia
Gerard
Gerrie
Gertie
Gertrude
Gina
Ginger
Ginnie
Ginny
Gloria
Golda

Grace
Gracey
Gracie
Greg
Greta
Gretchen
Guido
Gunther
Gussie
Gwen
Hailey
Haley
Hans
Harold
Harry
Harv
Harvey
Hattie
Hazel
Heather
Helen
Henry
Herbie
Herman
Hilary
Hilda

Hogan	Jean	Joel	Katelyn
Hollis	Jedgar	Joela	Katherine
Holly	Jeffrey	Joey	Kathryn
Howard	Jen	John	Kathy
Huey	Jenna	John Alex	Katie
Ian	Jennie	John Henry	Katy
Igor	Jennifer	Johnny	Kay
Ilsa	Jenny	Jonathan	Kelly
Inga	Jeremy	Jones	Kent
Ingrid	Jerry	Joni	Kerry
Ira	Jess	Jonie	Kevin
Irving	Jesse	Jordan	Kim
Isa	Jessica	Joseph	Kimberly
Ivan	Jessie	Josephine	Kimbrey
Jack	Jezabel	Josh	Kit
Jackie	Jill	Josie	Kristen
Jacob	Jim	Joya	Kristie
Jacques	Jimmie	Joyce	Kristy
Jake	Jimmy	Judy	Lacey
James	Joan	Jules	Lacie
Jamie	Joann	Julia	Lance
Jan	Joanne	Julie	Lanna
Jane	Jock	Julius	Larry
Janie	Jodie	Justin	Laura
Jason	Jody	Karen	Lauren
Jasper	Joe	Kate	Lea

Human Names

Leanne	Lou	Marlene	Michael
Lee	Louie	Marsha	Michelle
Leland	Louis	Marshie	Mickey
Lena	Louise	Martha	Mike
Leroy	Lucas	Martin	Mikey
Lesley	Lucy	Marvin	Miles
Leslie	Luigi	Mathilda	Millie
Lester	Luke	Matt	Mindy
Lianna	Maddy	Matthew	Mira
Libby	Madeline	Mattie	Miriam
Lilli	Maggie	Maude	Missy
Lilly	Magnum	Maudie	Misty
Linda	Malcolm	Maureen	Mitch
Lindsay	Mandy	Maven	Molly
Lisa	Mangus	Mavis	Monique
Liz	Marcey	Max	Montgomery
Liza	Marcia	Maxine	Monty
Lizzy	Marcie	May	Morris
Lois	Marcus	Maynard	Muriel
Lola	Marge	McGee	Murphy
Lolita	Margie	Meagan	Murray
Lollie	Margo	Meg	Nadine
Lora	Maria	Megan	Nance
Loren	Marianne	Melissa	Nancy
Lori	Marie	Melvin	Naomi
Lottie	Mark	Mia	Natalie

Nathan	Patrick	Reba	Ryan
Ned	Patty	Rebecca	Sabre
Neil	Paula	Reginald	Sabrina
Nell	Pearl	Rene	Sadie
Nellie	Peg	Renee	Sally
Nelly	Penelope	Rex	Sam
Newt	Percival	Rhett	Samantha
Nicholas	Percy	Rick	Sammy
Nick	Pete	Ricky	Sandy
Nicky	Petey	Riley	Sara
Nicole	Petra	Rita	Sarah
Niki	Petula	Robert	Sasha
Noel	Phil	Robin	Saul
Nora	Philip	Roger	Schroder
Norman	Phoebe	Ron	Schultz
Olin	Phyllis	Ronald	Scott
Olive	Polly	Ronney	Scottie
Oliver	Pollyanna	Ronnie	Sean
Ollie	Priscilla	Roscoe	Sebastian
Oscar	Prudy	Rose	Seth
Otto	Rachel	Roxanne	Seymour
Pam	Ralph	Roy	Shannon
Pamela	Randolph	Rudy	Sharon
Panchito	Randy	Russell	Shawn
Pancho	Raquel	Rusty	Shayne
Parker	Raymond	Ruth	Sheila

Shelby	Sylvia	Tom	Wally
Shelly	Tabitha	Tommy	Walter
Sherry	Tamara	Tony	Warren
Shirley	Tammy	Tracy	Wayne
Sibyl	Tanya	Travis	Webster
Sid	Taylor	Trenton	Wendy
Sidney	Ted	Trevor	Wilbur
Sophie	Teddy	Trish	William
Stacey	Teena	Trudy	Willie
Stanley	Templeton	Tucker	Willy
Stella	Teresa	Tyler	Wilma
Stephanie	Teri	Valerie	Windy
Stephen	Tessi	Van	Winnie
Steven	Tessie	Vanessa	Winston
Stuart	Theodore	Vaughan	Woodrow
Sue	Thomas	Vera	Wylie
Susan	Tiffany	Vic	Yvette
Susie	Timmy	Vick	Yvonne
Susy	Timothy	Vicky	Zachary
Suzanne	Tina	Victor	Zane
Suzette	Toby	Vincent	Zeke
Suzie	Todd	Virgil	Zoe
Suzy	Toddy	Virginia	

"Cleo"

"Honey Bunny"

CHAPPTER 4

Terms of Endearment

I am driven to the conclusion that my sense of kinship with animals is greater than most people feel. It amuses me to talk to animals in a sort of jargon I have invented for them; and it seems to me that it amuses them to be talked to, and they respond to the tone of the conversation, though its intellectual content may to some extent escape them.

George Bernard Shaw
from *Killing for Sport*

Many people use terms of endearment to refer to members of their families. A large number of people also use such terms when addressing their pets. Names such as "Baby" and "Sweetie" may not have originally been a dog's or cat's name, but through repeated use, an owner may come to refer to his or her pet in that manner. Many owners, however, choose a term of endearment for a special pet's name right away, and these names are often nearest and dearest to his or her heart.

Terms of Endearment

Ace
Angel
Babe
Baby
Baby Bear
Baby Cakes
Baby Doll
Baby Girl
Baby Kitty
Beau Beau
Bitsie
Bitsy
Bubby
Buffer
Cutsie
Dickens
Duster
Dusty
Fifi

Fluffer
Fu Fu
Fuffy
Gin Gin
Ginger Sugar
Gingi Girl
Girly
Good Boy
Good Girl
Hey Girl
Honey
Honey Blue
Honey Bunny
Honey Dew
Hot Dog
Hotlips
Itsy-Bitsy
Junior
Keeper

Kissy Bear
Kissy Face
Kitter
Lad
Laddie
Lov-a-Lot
Lover Boy
Lover Girl
Lovey
Lovey Lou
Lovums
Marshmallow
Nuffin
Patty Cake
Precious
Pudden
Puddin'
Puddy Tat
Punkin

Purdy
Sugar
Sugar 'n Spice
Sugar Baby
Sugar Bear
Sugar Pie
Sugar Plum
Sugarfoot
Sugarkins
Sunshine
Suzie Q
Sweet Pea
Sweet Thing
Sweetie
Sweetie Pie
Sweetums
Tootsie
True Blue

"Marshmallow"

"Washington"

CHAPTER 5

Historical Names

I never have been able to get very far in the exploration of the minds of people who call their dogs Mussolini, Tojo, and Adolf, and I suspect the reason is that I am unable to associate with them long enough to examine what goes on in their heads. I nod, and I tell them the time of day, if they ask, and that is all.

James Thurber
from *How to Name a Dog*

Many owners choose historical names for their pets, either because they enjoy history, because a particular historical figure interests them, or a pet actually resembles a well-known character from history. For instance, the name "Napoleon Bonaparte" could accurately describe a small, feisty dog. This chapter contains the names of some famous—and some infamous—dogs and cats of the past and a sampling of the names of the prominent figures of world history. The list of the latter is by no means complete—it only illustrates some of the names that other pet owners have used.

Historical Names

Aesop	A Greek writer of fables; lived during the late sixth century B.C.
Agrippina	The mother of the Roman emperor NERO. He had her murdered.
Alexander	(1) The name of three of the Russian czars. (2) Alexander of Macedonia, conqueror of the ancient world, who was known as "Alexander the Great."
Ambrose (Saint)	A bishop of Milan in the fourth century A.D. who was one of the most influential men of his time.
Appleseed, Johnny	John Chapman (1774–1845). The orchards of the Midwest grew from the seed that this nurseryman was reported to have spread across the land.
Aristotle	One of the greatest Greek thinkers and philosophers (384–322 B.C.) whose writings have had a major influence on the world.
Ashcroft (John)	Attorney General under the Bush administration.
Attila	King of Huns called the "Scourge of God" by peoples he conquered during the fifth century.
Aztec	The Aztecs were a group of people that originated in northwest Mexico, becoming a small nomadic tribe in the twelfth century, eventually expanding into a huge empire.
Bailey (James A.)	The British circus proprietor who merged with P. T. Barnum's traveling circus in 1881.

Balto	A black, long-haired malamute that in February, 1925 led Gunnar Kasson's dog team through a blizzard to reach diphtheria-plagued Nome, Alaska with antitoxin serum. A statue of Balto stands in New York City's Central Park.
Barnum (P. T.)	Phineas Taylor Barnum (1810–1891), co-founder of "The Barnum and Bailey Greatest Show on Earth."
Beau	General Omar BRADLEY'S pet poodle.
Beauregard	A Confederate general whose full name was Pierre Gustave Toutant de Beauregard.
Bessie	A collie that belonged to President Calvin Coolidge, the thirtieth President of the United States (1923–1929).
Big Ben	The fox terrier that belonged to President Herbert Hoover, named for the famous London clock.
Billy the Kid	William Bonney (1859–1881). A ruthless Wild West criminal who killed a man before reaching his teens.
Bingo	The black-and-white dog on Cracker Jack boxes.
Bismarck	Otto Eduard Leopold von Bismarck (1815–1898), a Prussian statesman who united the German states into one empire and created the Triple Alliance between Germany, Austria-Hungary, and Italy, thus preserving peace in Europe until World War I.
Blackberry	One of President Calvin Coolidge's pet dogs.
Blackie	A mixed-breed dog that belonged to the author when he was a child.

Historical Names

Blacky	President Calvin Coolidge's black cat.
Blair (Tony)	British Prime Minister.
Blanco	A white collie that a little girl in Illinois gave to President Lyndon B. Johnson during his term in office.
Bluegrass	Daniel BOONE'S family cat.
Bonham	A hero of the Battle of the Alamo (1836).
Boone (Daniel)	Hero of the early West who was a famous Indian fighter and frontiersman.
Bradley (Omar Nelson)	An American general who commanded troops in Europe in World War II.
Brutus	The Roman general and orator who led the plot to murder Julius Caesar in 44 B.C.
Buddy	The female German shepherd who was the first Seeing Eye dog. Buddy belonged to Morris Frank, a blind man from Tennessee, and was trained in Switzerland at the kennels where Dorothy Harrison Eustis, the founder of The Seeing Eye Inc., worked. Frank told Buddy's story in his book, *First Lady of Seeing Eye*.
Buddy	A Labrador Retriever that belonged to former President Clinton.
Buffalo Bill	William Cody (1846–1917), was a famous hunter and scout who starred in and operated his own Wild West show.
Bush (George)	The forty-first President of the United States.

Bush (George W.)   The forty-third President of the United States.

Bush (Laura)   The first lady, wife of President George W. Bush.

Caesar (Julius)   The Roman general and statesman who became dictator of Rome, ending the era of the Roman Republic.

Charlemagne   The great military leader who became the first Holy Roman Emperor from A.D. 800–814.

Charlie   One of President John F. Kennedy's dogs.

Checkers   A black-and-white cocker spaniel sent to Richard Nixon when he was running for vice president. Nixon revealed Checkers' existence when he appeared on television on September 23, 1952, to combat allegations that he had received illegal campaign funds. His speech has since been called the Checkers Speech.

Cheney (Dick)   Vice President of the United States.

Chips   A shepherd-husky-collie mix that was the first member of the army's K-9 Corps sent overseas in World War II. Chips landed in Sicily in July 1943 and aided pinned-down American troops by attacking Italian gunners. He received decorations for this act and returned home in 1945.

Cicero   The statesman and orator who tried to save the dying Roman Republic.

Cleopatra   The name for the seven queens of ancient Egypt. The most famous was Cleopatra VII (69–30 B.C.), who was the subject of many literary works, including Shakespeare's *Antony and Cleopatra* and *Caesar and Cleopatra* by George Bernard Shaw.

Historical Names

Cloe

A dog that belonged to George WASHINGTON, first President of the United States (1789–1797).

Cochise

Chief of the central Chiricahua in Southeastern Arizona (1800–1874), the most famous Apache leader to resist intrusions by whites.

Constantine

Flavius Valerius Constantinus (A.D. 280–337); also known as Constantine the Great, the first Roman emperor to adopt Christianity.

Crockett (Davy)

Famous frontiersman who died at the Battle of the Alamo (1836).

Cuba

One of Ernest Hemingway's forty cats.

Custer (George Armstrong)

The famous American army officer who lost his life in a battle against the Indians at Little Bighorn, which has become known as Custer's Last Stand.

Dubya

George W. Bush's nickname.

Durkheim (Emile)

The French sociologist and founder (1859–1917) of modern sociology as an academic discipline.

Einstein (Albert)

The German-American physicist (1879–1955) who published the Theory of Relativity in 1905.

Fala

The Scottish terrier that Franklin D. Roosevelt humorously defended against unjustified attacks by his political opponents.

Ferdinand

A king of Spain who, with his wife Isabella, received Christopher Columbus at the Court in Barcelona and agreed to finance his voyage.

Fido	The yellow mongrel belonging to Abraham Lincoln's two sons, Willie and Tad. Fido stayed behind in Springfield, Illinois when the President-elect and his family moved to Washington.
Freebo	One of six dogs owned by President Ronald Reagan during his presidency.
Freud (Sigmund)	The famous psychoanalyst (1856–1939) whose work profoundly affected the study and practice of psychology and psychiatry.
Galilei (Galileo)	Italian astronomer, mathematician, and physicist (1564–1642).
Gandhi (Mohandas Karamchand)	The great Indian statesman (1869–1948) who freed his county from British rule through nonviolent resistance. Gandhi is considered the father of modern India.
Gates (Bill)	CEO of the Microsoft corporation; multi-billionaire.
Genghis Khan	The great Mongol ruler (1167–1227) who conquered a vast empire, including China.
Geronimo	Apache Indian leader (1829–1909) who eventually became a rancher. While in St. Louis for the Louisiana Purchase Exposition, he rode in President Theodore Roosevelt's inaugural parade in 1905.
Gingrich (Newt)	Speaker of the House under the Clinton Administration.
Golda Meir	The woman who became Prime Minister of Israel in 1969.
Gorbachev (Mikhail)	Soviet leader (b. 1931) from 1985 to 1991.

Historical Names

Grant (Ulysses S.) Union general during the Civil War and the eighteenth President of the United States.

Greenspan (Alan) Chairman of the Federal Reserve.

Grits The dog belonging to President Jimmy Carter's daughter, Amy.

Handsome Dan The white bulldog that was the original Yale bulldog mascot. The first Handsome Dan has been followed by a series of namesakes, one of which still represents Yale today.

Heidi A Weimaraner owned by President Dwight D. Eisenhower.

Her One of the pair of beagles that accompanied President Lyndon B. Johnson and his family to the White House. Johnson received much criticism when he lifted Her and the other beagle HIM up by the ears.

Him The other half of President Lyndon B. Johnson's pair of beagles. (See HER)

Hitler (Adolf) The totalitarian ruler of Germany's Third Reich who initiated World War II and was responsible for the slaughter of millions of people.

Houdini (Harry) The famous magician (1874–1926) who could escape from any contraption devised to hold him.

Igloo The troublesome fox terrier that traveled with Admiral Richard E. Byrd on his first trip to the Antarctic (1928–1930).

Ike The nickname of Dwight David Eisenhower, the Supreme Commander of the Allied armies in Europe in World War II. Eisenhower later became President of the United States (1953–1961).

Isabella	Queen of Spain and wife of FERDINAND.
Ivan	The name of several Russian rulers. Ivan IV (1533–1584), known as "Ivan the Terrible," was the first Russian czar.
Jackson (Stonewall)	The Confederate general during the Civil War, second only to General Robert E. Lee.
James (Jesse)	The notorious bank and train robber who vandalized the American West during the nineteenth century.
Jo-Fi	Psychoanalyst Sigmund Freud's beloved chow.
King Timahoe	The Irish setter owned by President Richard Nixon.
King Tut	President Herbert Hoover's pet German shepherd dog.
Kublai Khan	Mongol emperor (c. 1216–1294), who was the grandson of Genghis Khan.
Laddie Boy	The Airedale that belonged to President Warren G. Harding.
Lady	One of George WASHINGTON's pet dogs.
Laika	The female Samoyed that was the first living creature to orbit the earth in the second Soviet Sputnik.
Lee (Robert E.)	Famous general of the Confederacy during the Civil War.
Lewinsky (Monica)	Former White House intern involved in sex scandal with former President Clinton.

Historical Names

Liberty — President Gerald Ford's golden retriever.

Livingstone (David) — A famous British explorer who pioneered large parts of Africa during the nineteenth century.

Lucky — A black sheepdog owned by President Ronald Reagan. Of the six of President Reagan's dogs, only two resided at the White House—Lucky and REX.

Magellan (Ferdinand) — The Portuguese navigator who was the first person to sail around the world.

Major — A German shepherd that belonged to Franklin Delano Roosevelt.

Mao Tse-tung (Zedong) — One of the founders of the Chinese Communist Party in 1921 and the People's Republic of China in 1949.

Marco — A Pomeranian that belonged to Queen Victoria of England.

Marco Polo — A Venetian who was one of the first Europeans to travel in Asia during the late thirteenth century.

Marjorie — A diabetic black-and-white mongrel that was the first creature to be kept alive by insulin.

Maximilian — The Austrian whom the French installed as emperor of the short-lived Mexican throne (1864–1867).

Meggy — One of Franklin D. Roosevelt's pet dogs. FALA was Meggy's sire.

Mendel (Gregor) — Augustinian monk known as the father of genetics.

Merlin
The wizard and counselor of King Arthur from *The Tales of King Arthur and His Court.*

Micetto
Pepe Leo XII's large black-striped cat. After the Pope's death, the cat went to live with the French ambassador to Rome, the Vicomte de Chateaubriand.

Millie
(1) A mixed breed dog (part Irish setter, part collie) owned by President Ronald Reagan. (2) The English springer spaniel belonging to President and Mrs. George Bush. Mrs. Bush wrote a book about Millie.

Ming
The dynasty that ruled China from 1368 to 1644. The Ming period was one of artistic growth.

Montgomery (Bernard Law)
The British general who won fame during the African campaign and the invasion of Europe in World War II.

Mopsey
One of George WASHINGTON'S favorite dogs.

Moshe Dayan
A leading Israeli general and statesman (1915–1981).

Mushka
A dog that was placed in orbit by the Russians in one of the first Sputnik space vehicles.

Napoleon (Bonaparte)
The French general and military genius (1769–1821) who crowned himself Emperor of France and conquered much of Europe.

Neff (Pat)
A governor of Texas during the first half of the twentieth century and a president of Baylor University in Waco, Texas.

Nelson	A black cat, the favorite of Sir Winston Churchill, Prime Minister of Great Britain during most of World War II.
Nelson (Horatio)	Great Britain's greatest admiral and naval hero, who established Britain's rule of the seas in the 1800s.
Nero	One of the cruelest Roman emperors, who killed thousands of Christians.
Newton (Sir Isaac)	The English scientist, astronomer, and mathematician (1642–1727) who invented calculus and first established the laws of gravity.
Niña, Pinta, and Santa Maria	The three ships in Christopher Columbus's fleet when he discovered America on October 12, 1492.
Nipper	The fox terrier that appears with a phonograph in the RCA trademark.
Nobel (Alfred)	Invented dynamite and established the Nobel Prize which is awarded every year for excellence in many fields.
Patton (George Smith)	An American general (1885–1945) who led the 3rd Army in Europe during World War II.
Pavlov (Ivan Petrovich)	The Russian physiologist who won the 1904 Nobel Prize in physiology and medicine for his research on conditioned reflexes.
Perruque	One of fourteen cats owned by Cardinal Richelieu when he died in 1642.
Plato	A famous Greek philosopher (c.428–c.348 B.C.) who was a follower of Socrates.

Pompey the Great	Roman general and statesman (106–48 B.C.) who was one of Julius Caesar's greatest adversaries.
Pompidou (Georges)	Premier and President (1911–1974) of France's Fifth Republic from 1962–1974.
Powell (Colin)	Secretary of State under the Bush Administration.
Princess Diana	Born Diana Spencer in 1961, she married Prince Charles in 1981. She lived a high-profile life until her tragic and untimely death in 1997.
Pushinka	A puppy from STRELKA'S litter that the Soviet Premier Nikita Khrushchev presented to Mrs. John F. Kennedy when she was First Lady.
Rasputin	The religious man (1865–1916) who corrupted Russia's Czar Nicholas II and his wife Alexandra.
Reagan (Ronald)	The motion picture actor and California governor who became the fortieth President of the United States.
Reno (Janet)	Attorney General under the Clinton Administration.
Rex	A spaniel that belonged to President Ronald Reagan.
Ripley (Robert Leroy)	An American cartoonist who began collecting strange and unusual facts that he eventually compiled into two *Believe It or Not* books.
Rob Roy	President Calvin Coolidge's white collie.

Historical Names

Rommel (Erwin)	The brilliant German general (1891–1994) who commanded the Afrika Korps and the forces defending Normandy in World War II.
Ross (Betsy)	Creator of the first U.S. flag.
Rover	The collie that was President Lyndon Johnson's first dog.
Rufus	A poodle owned by British Prime Minister Winston Churchill.
Rumsfeld (Donald)	Secretary of Defense under the Bush Administration.
Sailor Boy	Theodore Roosevelt's pet dog.
Scannon	Meriwether Lewis's black Newfoundland that accompanied the Lewis and Clark expedition to the Pacific.
Searcher	One of George WASHINGTON'S pet dogs.
Shannon	A dog that was the White House pet of John F. Kennedy, Jr.
Sharon (Ariel)	Prime Minister of Israel.
Shasta	The first U.S.-born *liger*, the offspring of a male lion and a female tiger, to reach maturity. Shasta was born May 6, 1948, at the Hogle Zoological Garden in Salt Lake City, Utah.
Sherman (William Tecumseh)	The famous Union general during the American Civil War.
Sizi	The cat that was a companion to Albert Schweitzer (1875–1965) when he was a medical missionary in Africa.

Skip	A mongrel dog owned by President Theodore Roosevelt.
Socks	A cat that belonged to former President Clinton.
Socrates	A noted Greek philosopher (470–399 B.C.) whose beliefs included justice and good moral character.
Stanley (Henry)	The British explorer who led the expedition to find David LIVINGSTONE.
Strelka	One of the two female Samoyeds that the Soviet Union launched in Sputnik V on August 19, 1960.
Taca	A Siberian husky owned by President Ronald Reagan.
Thatcher (Margaret)	The former Prime Minister of Great Britain who was known as the "Iron Lady."
Thurmond (Strom)	Currently 100 years of age, the oldest member of the U.S. Senate (South Carolina, Republican).
Tito	The Communist ruler of Yugoslavia after World War II. Tito declared Yugoslavia's independence from Soviet control.
Trafalgar	The cape on Spain's southern coast at the western entrance to the Strait of Gibraltar that was the sight of one of history's greatest naval battles: Great Britain, led by Admiral Horatio Nelson, defeated the combined French and Spanish fleets on October 21, 1805.
Traveler	The horse of Robert E. Lee, the Confederate general during the American Civil War.

Historical Names

Trojan	An inhabitant of Troy, an ancient city in Asia Minor that Homer made famous.
Uncle Sam	The personification of the United States; his top hat and red, white, and blue clothes make him a distinctive figure.
Victory	A golden retriever owned by President Ronald Reagan.
Viking	A member of the Scandinavian bands of sea rovers who raided England, Ireland, France, Germany, Italy, and Spain between the 700s and 1100s. The Vikings also settled Greenland and Iceland.
Voltaire	Eighteenth-century French man of letters; defended those unjustly persecuted by the Church.
Washington (George)	Commander of the American forces during the Revolutionary War and first President of the United States.
Watson	(1) Alexander Graham Bell's assistant. (2) Sherlock Holmes' friend and assistant in the Arthur Conan Doyle fictional mysteries.
Winston (Churchill)	The Prime Minister of Great Britain from 1940 to 1945 and from 1951 to 1955, who was one of the world's greatest statesmen.
Wright (Orville and Wilbur)	Credited with flying the first airplane at Kitty Hawk, North Carolina, December 17, 1903.
Yeltsin (Boris)	Former Russian President and Nobel Prize winner.
Yuki	The small white dog adopted by President Lyndon B. Johnson in November 1966. Yuki quickly became the President's favorite dog.
Zedillo (Ernesto)	Former Mexican President.

"Winston"

ATHENA

CHAPTER 6

Greek and Roman Mythology

Far from Italy, far from my native Tarentum I lie;
And this is the worst of it—worse than death.
An exile's life is no life. But the Muses loved me.
For my suffering they gave me a honeyed gift:
My name survives me. Thanks to the Sweet Muses.
Leonidas will echo through all time.

Leonidas of Tarentum
from *The Greek Anthology*

The gods, goddesses, and other figures of mythology are known for both their colorful appearance and their vibrant personalities; furthermore, they generally have unusual, and therefore, memorable names. Thus, pets often are namesakes of these characters, and a pet's mythological name can provide a great source of conversation.

Achelous	A River God who turned himself into a bull to fight Heracles (see HERCULES) because the two men were both in love with the same woman, Deianira.
Achilles	The champion of the Greeks in the Trojan War.
Actaeon	A young hunter whom ARTEMIS turned into a stag because he had accidentally seen her naked. In his new form, Actaeon's own dogs chased and killed him.
Adonis	APHRODITE'S love, who spent half the year with her and the other half in the Underworld. A boar killed him, and a crimson flower sprung up where each drop of his blood fell.
Aeneas	The son of APHRODITE (Venus) who fought for TROY in the Trojan War. After the defeat he escaped to Italy where he founded the Roman race.
Aero	ORION'S love and the daughter of the King of Chios.
Aidos	The personified emotion of reverence and shame, which was esteemed highest of all feelings.
Ajax	One of the Greek champions in the Trojan War.
Alce	One of ACTAEON'S hounds; the name means "strength."
Alexander	Another name for PARIS, who caused the Trojan War and died of a wound from a poisoned arrow.
Althea	The mother of Meleager; she killed him and then killed herself.

Amazon	A member of the nation of women warriors who had no dealings with men except to oppose them in war and to breed children.
Andromeda	The daughter of CASSIOPEIA, who was punished for her mother's vanity. PERSEUS saved her from her fate, and she married him.
Antigone	The daughter of OEDIPUS. She was killed by CREON, his successor on the throne.
Aphrodite	The Goddess of Love and Beauty.
Apollo	The God of Light and Truth.
Arcas	The son of CALLISTO and ZEUS whom Zeus placed among the stars as Ursa Minor (Lesser Bear).
Ares	The God of War (Roman: Mars). The Son of ZEUS and HERA; he was a bully and also a coward, detested by his parents as well as others.
Argos	ODYSSEUS'S dog. After being away at Trojan War for twenty years, Odysseus returned to his home disguised as a beggar, and only Argos recognized him. The dog, too sick and weak to walk, wagged his tail in recognition; however, afraid of revealing his identity, Odysseus didn't acknowledge Argos, and as Odysseus walked on, Argos died.
Argus	HERA'S watchman with a hundred eyes.
Ariadne	King MINOS'S daughter who was deserted on the island of NAXOS by her lover, THESEUS.
Arion	The first horse, an offspring of POSEIDON.

Greek and Roman Mythology

Arne   Regarded as the ancestress of the Boeotian Greeks.

Artemis   The Goddess of Hunting and Wild Things.

Asbolos   One of ACTAEON'S hounds; the name means "soot-color."

Asopus   A River God.

Atalanta   The maiden who could outshoot, outrun, and outwrestle most men. She eventually was turned into a lioness.

Ate   The Goddess of Mischief. Although a daughter of ZEUS, she was cast out of OLYMPUS.

Athena   The Goddess of the City, Protector of Civilized Life, Handicrafts, and Agriculture.

Atlas   The TITAN who held the world on his shoulders.

Attica   The country around Athens.

Aurora   The Goddess of Dawn.

Bacchus   Roman name for DIONYSUS, the God of the Vine.

Banos   One of ACTAEON'S hounds.

Battus   A peasant who saw HERMES steal APOLLO'S cattle. Hermes turned Battus into stone because the man broke his promise not to reveal the identity of the thief to Apollo.

Baucis   A poor old woman who was blessed by the gods, given a temple to live in, and promised that she would never live alone without her husband.

Bellona	The Roman name for ENYO, the Goddess of War.
Belus	The grandfather of the Danaïds (who were condemned to carry water in jars that were forever leaking).
Biton	One of the two sons of Cydippe, a priestess of HERA. He and his brother yoked themselves to a wagon to carry their mother to pray. The journey killed both sons.
Boötes	The constellation just behind the Dipper. See ICARIUS.
Boreas	(1) The God of the North Wind who kidnapped and ravished Orithyia. (2) One of ACTAEON'S hounds.
Bromius	Another name for DIONYSUS, who was a son of ZEUS. (See BACCHUS.)
Brontes	One of three CYCLOPS, each of whom had only one eye in the middle of his forehead.
Cabeiri	Dwarfs with supernatural powers. They protected the fields of Lemnos.
Cacus	The giant who stole cattle from Heracles' (HERCULES') flock.
Calliope	The daughter of ZEUS who was the MUSE of Epic Poetry.
Callisto	LYCAON'S daughter who was seduced by ZEUS and bore him a son, ARCAS. In a jealous rage, HERA turned Callisto into a bear, and when Arcas grew up placed his mother before him so that he would kill her. Zeus, however, saved Callisto and put her up in the stars as Ursa Major (Great Bear), placing Arcas beside her as Ursa Minor (Lesser Bear).

Calpe	The ancient Greek name for the Rock of Gibraltar.
Calypso	A nymph who kept ODYSSEUS prisoner on her island.
Camilla	A very skilled maiden warrior who was followed by a band of warriors.
Canache	One of ACTAEON'S hounds; the name means "ringwood."
Cassandra	One of PRIAM'S daughters. She became a prophetess because APOLLO loved her and gave her power of prognostication. Unfortunately, her prophecies were never believed.
Castor	The brother of POLLUX and the son of LEDA. He and his brother were the Protectors of Sailors.
Centaur	A creature who was half man and half horse.
Cerberus	The huge, fearsome watchdog of HADES. Cerberus guarded the gates of Hades, preventing spirits from leaving.
Ceres	The Roman name for DEMETER.
Chaos	The Nothingness that existed before the gods and before Creation.
Charites	Another name for the Graces who attended APHRODITE.
Charon	The boatman who guided the ferry that carried the dead souls to the gates of HADES.
Chediatros	One of ACTAEON'S hounds.
Circe	A beautiful and dangerous witch who turned men into beasts.

Cisseta	One of ACTAEON'S hounds.
Cleobis	BITON'S brother, son of Cydippe, a priestess of HERA. Cleobis perished with his brother after they yoked themselves to a wagon carrying their mother to pray.
Clio	The MUSE of History.
Clytie	A maiden who loved the Sun God, but whose love was not returned. She stared at him with longing until she turned into a sunflower.
Cora	Another name for PERSEPHONE.
Coran	One of ACTAEON'S hounds; the name means "crop-eared."
Coronis	A maiden whom APOLLO loved, but who did not love him. She was unfaithful, so he killed her.
Cottus	A monster with a hundred hands.
Creon	The brother of JOCASTA. Creon became regent after OEDIPUS resigned the throne.
Cronus	A titan who was the father of ZEUS.
Cupid	Latin for EROS, the Greek God of Love.
Cyclops	A giant with only one eye in the middle of his forehead.
Cyllo	One of ACTAEON'S hounds; the name means "halt."
Cyllopotes	One of ACTAEON'S hounds; the name means "zigzagger."

Cynthia   Another name for ARTEMIS.

Cyprian   Another name for APHRODITE.

Cyprios   One of ACTAEON'S hounds.

Cyprus   The island where APHRODITE was born.

Dactyls   The women of Mount Ida, who were the first to make implements of iron.

Daphne   A huntress whose father, the River God Peneus, changed her into a tree to protect her from APOLLO who loved her.

Delian   Another name for APOLLO.

Delos   The island where APOLLO was born and where his temple stood.

Delphi   The site of APOLLO'S oracles.

Demeter   The Goddess of Corn. Sister of ZEUS, she bore him a daughter, PERSEPHONE.

Diana   The Roman name for ARTEMIS.

Dido   The founder and queen of Carthage. She threw herself on a pyre when AENEAS, whom she loved, left to search for a homeland in Italy.

Diomedes   A great Greek warrior at TROY.

Dione   A minor goddess. By some accounts, Dione and Zeus were APHRODITE'S parents.

Dirce	The wife of LYCUS, the ruler of THEBES. Her grandsons and daughter killed her by tying her hair to a bull.
Dodona	ZEUS'S oracle, the oldest in Greece.
Dorian	A member of one of the principal groups of ancient Greeks.
Doris	One of the 3,000 daughters of Ocean and wife NEREUS.
Draco	One of ACTAEON'S hounds; the name means "the dragon."
Dromas	One of ACTAEON'S hounds; the name means "the courser."
Dromios	One of ACTAEON'S hounds; the name means "seize 'em."
Dryad	One of the nymphs of the trees.
Echnobas	One of ACTAEON'S hounds.
Echo	The fairest of the nymphs who loved NARCISSUS; HERA condemned her never to talk unless she repeated what someone else had already said.
Electra	The daughter of Agamemnon and Clytemnestra. She avenged her father's murder by inciting her brother, ORESTES, to kill their mother and her lover.
Enyo	The Goddess of War.
Erato	The MUSE of Love Poetry.
Erigone	The daughter of ICARIUS, who hanged herself after finding her father murdered. DIONYSUS placed her in the heavens as Virgo.

Eris	The sister of ARES whose name means "discord."
Eros	The God of Love.
Eudromos	One of ACTAEON'S hounds; the name means "good runner."
Europa	A maiden with whom ZEUS fell in love. As a bull, he carried her off to Crete. The continent of Europe was named for her.
Eurus	The God of the East Wind.
Fauna	The Roman Goddess of Fertility, sometimes called the Good Goddess.
Favonius	The Latin name for the West Wind.
Flora	The Roman Flower Goddess.
Galatea	(1) A sea nymph whom Polyphemus, the cyclops, loved. (2) The name of PYGMALION'S statue, which came to life.
Gemini	The constellation of the twin brothers, CASTOR and POLLUX.
Gorgon	Dragonlike creatures with wings and snakes for hair, whose look turned men to stone.
Hades	The God of the Underworld. He was the son of CRONUS and RHEA. (Hades is also used as a name for the Underworld itself.)
Harmonia	Cadmus's wife, who was the daughter of ARES and APHRODITE.
Harpale	One of ACTAEON'S hounds; the name means "voracious."

Hebe	The Goddess of Youth. She was the daughter of ZEUS and HERA.
Hecate	A triple deity who was Goddess of the Moon, Goddess of the Earth, and Goddess of the Underworld.
Hector	The brave, noble son of King PRIAM of TROY. Hector was the Trojan champion in the Trojan War.
Hecuba	The queen of TROY and wife of King PRIAM.
Helen	The daughter of ZEUS and LEDA, who was the fairest woman in the world. She married MENELAUS, but PARIS kidnapped her, starting the Trojan War.
Helicon	One of the MUSES' mountains. It was sacred to APOLLO whose temple was there.
Helios	The Sun God.
Hephaestus	The God of Fire.
Hera	ZEUS'S wife and sister. She was the Protector of Marriage and Married Women.
Heracles	See HERCULES.
Hercules	The Roman name for HERACLES, Greece's greatest hero and the strongest man alive.
Hermes	ZEUS'S messenger. He was sometimes called the "Master Thief."
Hermione	Unaware she had been promised to Orestes, MENELAUS gave her to ACHILLES' son, Pyrrhus.

Hero	The ill-fated lover of LEANDER. He died, and she killed herself.
Herse	An Athenian princess who was beloved by Hermes.
Hesper	The Goddess of the Evening Star.
Hesperides	The daughter of ATLAS, who with LADON (2), guarded the trees with golden branches, golden leaves, and golden apples.
Hestia	The Goddess of the Hearth.
Hilara	The daughter of APOLLO. Her name means "laughter-loving."
Himeros	The God of Desire who attended EROS. Also called Longing.
Hippodamia	Wife of PELOPS. He won her in a chariot race.
Hippolytus	The son of THESEUS whose second wife, PHAEDRA, fell in love with Hippolytus.
Hyacinth	A companion of APOLLO. He was accidentally killed when Apollo's discus hit him in the head. On each spot where a drop of his blood fell, a Hyacinth flower arose.
Hyades	Some nymphs whom ZEUS placed as the stars that bring rain when they are near the horizon.
Hydra	A nine-headed creature killed by HERACLES. (See HERCULES.)
Hypnos	The God of Sleep.
Iacchus	Another name for DIONYSUS. (See BACCHUS.)

Ibycus	A poet who lived around 550 B.C. When robbers left him mortally wounded he asked the cranes that were flying overhead to avenge him, and they did.
Icarus	The son of Daedalus, the architect. When Icarus flew too near the sun, the wax that held his wings in place melted. Icarus fell to earth and was killed.
Icarius	An Athenian, in Greek mythology, whom DIONYSUS taught how to make wine. Drunken shepherds murdered Icarius and threw him down a well, where his faithful dog, MAERA, found him. Dionysus honored Icarius, placing him among the stars as the constellation BOÖTES.
Icelus	The son of HYPNOS, who had the power to change himself into all sorts of birds and animals.
Ichnobate	One of ACTAEON'S hounds; the name means "tracker."
Ida	A nymph who took care of ZEUS when he was being hidden from Cronus.
Inachus	The father of IO.
Ino	The Sea Goddess who saved ODYSSEUS from drowning.
Io	The maiden who had an affair with ZEUS. He turned her into a white heifer to protect her from HERA'S jealous wrath. Unfortunately, Io, wound up in Hera's possession and spent years trying to escape and return to her original form. Finally, Zeus restored Io's humanity, and she spent the rest of her days happily.
Iphicles	Heracles' (HERCULES) half brother.

Iris	The Goddess of the Rainbow.
Ixion	The first murderer. Ixion also attempted to seduce HERA. ZEUS sentenced him to eternal punishment in HADES, where he was tied to a wheel and lashed with serpents.
Janus	A NUMINA who became personified. Janus was the God of Good Beginnings.
Jason	The leader of the quest for the GOLDEN FLEECE.
Jocasta	OEDIPUS'S mother and wife.
Jove	Another name for ZEUS.
Juna	The Roman name for HERA.
Jupiter	The Roman name for ZEUS.
Juturna	The Roman Goddess of Springs.
Kora	Another name for PERSEPHONE.
Labros	One of ACTAEON'S hounds; the name means "furious."
Lacena	One of ACTAEON'S hounds; the name means "lioness."
Lachne	One of ACTAEON'S hounds; the name means "glossy."
Lacon	One of ACTAEON'S hounds.

Ladon	(1) One of ACTAEON'S hounds. (2) The serpent who guarded the Golden Apples of the HESPERIDES.
Laertes	ODYSSEUS'S father.
Laius	The father of OEDIPUS. Oedipus unwittingly murdered him.
Lampos	One of ACTAEON'S hounds; the name means "shining one."
Lar	A NUMINA, who was the spirit of an ancestor. Every Roman family had a Lar.
Larvae	The spirits of HADES'S wicked dead, who were greatly feared.
Latinus	The great-grandson of SATURN and the king of the city of LATIUM.
Latium	A city in Italy that was conquered by AENEAS.
Latona	Another name for LETO.
Lavinia	The daughter of LATINUS and the wife of AENEAS. Together, husband and wife founded the Roman race.
Leander	HERO'S lover who killed herself after he drowned swimming to a rendezvous with her.
Leda	The wife of King Tyndareus of Sparta. ZEUS, in the form of a swan, seduced her.
Lelaps	(1) One of ACTAEON'S hounds; the name means "hurricane." (2) The hound destined to chase a fox until ZEUS finally changed them both to stone.

Lemures	Another name for LARVAE.
Lethe	The River of Forgetfulness in the Underworld.
Leto	Daughter of TITANS; APOLLO and ARTEMIS were her children by ZEUS.
Leucos	One of ACTAEON'S hounds; the name means "gray."
Liber	Another name for BACCHUS.
Libera	A Roman name for PERSEPHONE. She was abducted by PLUTO, who wanted her to be queen of the Underworld.
Libitina	The Roman Goddess of the Dead.
Linus	The son of APOLLO and Psamathe. When his mother deserted him, dogs tore him apart.
Lotis	A nymph who was changed into a lotus tree.
Lucina	Sometimes regarded as the Roman Goddess of Childbirth.
Luna	Latin for the Goddess of the Moon. The name Luna referred to DIANA.
Lyaeus	Another name for BACCHUS.
Lycaon	A king of ATTICA and the father of CALLISTO. When he served human flesh at a banquet, ZEUS turned him into a wolf.
Lycisca	One of ACTAEON'S hounds.

Lycus	Ruler of THEBES and the husband of DIRCE. His daughter killed him because of his cruelty.
Lyncea	One of ACTAEON'S hounds.
Machaon	The Greeks' physician during the Trojan War.
Machimos	One of ACTAEON'S hounds; the name means "boxer."
Maeander	River in Phrygia that frequently changes its course.
Maera	A faithful dog, whose master ICARIUS was murdered and thrown into a well. Maera led Icarius's daughter ERIGONE to the body. She hanged herself and the dog then jumped into the well.
Maia	VULCAN'S wife. (See HEPHATETUS.)
Manes	The spirits of the good dead in HADES.
Mars	Roman name for ARES.
Medea	The daughter of King Colchias. A sorceress, she fell in love with JASON and helped him on his quest for the GOLDEN FLEECE.
Medusa	One of the GORGONS. PERSEUS cut off her head.
Megara	The wife of Heracles (HERCULES) and mother of three of his sons. Hercules went mad and killed them all.
Melampus	A great soothsayer whose pet snakes taught him animal language.
Melanchete	One of ACTAEON'S hounds; the name means "black-coated."

Melanea	One of ACTAEON'S hounds; the name means "black."
Melanion	The runner who beat ATALANTA and won her love.
Melpomene	The MUSE of Tragedy.
Menelaus	The brother of Agamemnon and husband of HELEN.
Menelea	One of ACTAEON'S hounds.
Mentor	ODYSSSUS'S most trusted friend. ATHENA disguised herself as Mentor when she appeared to TELEMACHUS.
Mercury	The Roman name for HERMES.
Metis	ZEUS'S first wife, also called Prudence. Zeus swallowed her and developed a monumental headache, which eased only after ATHENA sprang from his head.
Midas	A king of Phrygia whose wish that everything he touched would turn to gold was granted.
Minerva	The Roman name for ATHENA.
Minos	One of the three judges in the Underworld.
Minotaur	A monster that was half bull and half human.
Minyas	The king of THESSALY. The ARGONAUTS, sometimes called the Minyae, were his descendants.

Moira	Fate, a mysterious power stronger than the gods. One who scorned Moira would meet NEMESIS.
Molossos	One of ACTAEON'S hounds.
Moly	An herb with white blossoms that HERMES gave ODYSSEUS to protect him from CIRCE'S spells.
Mopsus	Soothsayer of the ARGONAUTS, he also went on the Calydonian boar hunt.
Morpheus	The God of Sleep; also called the God of Dreams.
Mors	The God of Death; also called Thanatos.
Muse	One of nine daughters of ZEUS and Mnemosyne. They were goddesses of memory and then of the arts and sciences.
Myrmidon	One of a group of soldiers who fought against the TROJANS.
Napa	One of ACTAEON'S hounds; the name means "sired by a wolf."
Narcissus	A beautiful boy who scorned love despite many admiring ladies. Finally, he was cursed, fell in love with himself, and pined away for his own reflection in a pond.
Naxos	The island where THESEUS left ARIADNE.
Neleus	One of the twin sons of TYRO and POSEIDON.
Nemean Lion, The	The ferocious lion that ravaged the valley of Nemea, until Heracles (HERCULES) strangled the beast to death.

Greek and Roman Mythology

Nemesis	The Goddess of Righteous Anger, the personified emotion esteemed highest of all feelings.
Neptune	The Roman name for POSEIDON.
Nereid	A nymph of the sea and the daughter of NEREUS.
Nereus	The Old Man of the Sea. He had the power of prophecy and could assume any form he desired.
Nessus	A centaur who gave Heracles' (HERCULES') wife, Deianira, his blood as a love potion when he was dying.
Nestor	The wisest and oldest of the Greek chieftans.
Nike	The Greek Goddess of Victory.
Notus	The God of the South Wind.
Numina	The powers that were the Roman gods before the Romans adopted the Greek ones.
Ocydroma	One of ACTAEON'S hounds; the name means "swift runner."
Ocyrrhoe	A prophetess.
Odysseus	The Greek hero of the Trojan War, known for his cunning.
Oedipus	The king who was fated to kill his father and marry his mother.
Olympus	A mountain peak in Greece and home of the gods.

Ophion	A great serpent that ruled the TITANS before CRONUS.
Ops	The wife of SATURN (see CRONUS), who was the Goddess of the Harvest.
Orcus	The Roman name for the King of the Dead. (See HADES, PLUTO.)
Orestes	The son of Agamemnon and Clytemnestra. He avenged his father's murder by killing his mother and her lover.
Oribasos	One of ACTAEON'S hounds; the name means "mountain-ranger."
Orion	ARTEMIS'S hunter. After she killed him, he was placed in the sky as a constellation.
Orpheus	The greatest mortal musician. He journeyed to the Underworld to find his dead bride, EURYDICE.
Orthia	Another name for ARTEMIS.
Ossa	A mountain in THESSALY once inhabited by centaurs.
Otus	One of twin brothers, both giants, who wanted to prove themselves superior to the gods. ARTEMIS killed them for their presumption by making them accidentally kill each other.
Paean	The physician to the gods; also, APOLLO as healer.
Pales	The Strengthener of Cattle.
Palladium	The sacred image of ATHENA in TROY that protected the city as long as it was kept there.

Pamphagos   One of ACTAEON'S hounds; the name means "ravenous."

Pan   The God of the Goatherds and Shepherds who was part goat and part man.

Pandora   The first woman created by ZEUS; she brought evil into the world.

Panope   One of the sea nymphs.

Paphos   The daughter of the lovers PYGMALION and GALATEA, who gave her name to APHRODITE'S favorite city.

Paris   The TROJAN who kidnapped HELEN, starting the Trojan War.

Parthenon   ATHENA'S temple in Athens.

Pegasus   The winged horse that sprang from MEDUSA'S blood when PERSEUS killed her.

Peitho   The Goddess of Persuasion. She was the daughter of HERMES and APHRODITE.

Pelasgus   The ancestor of the Pelasgian—one of the earliest groups to inhabit the islands and mainland of Greece and Anaholia.

Peleus   ACHILLES' father. He was one of the ARGONAUTS.

Pelias   One of the twin sons of TYRO and POSEIDON.

Pelops   The son of TANTALUS. He was killed by his father, boiled in a cauldron, and served to the gods to eat.

Penates	The Gods of the Hearth and the Guardians of the Storehouse.
Penelope	ODYSSEUS'S faithful wife.
Pentheus	King of THEBES who was killed by the Bacchae when he was caught watching their secret rites.
Pergamos	The holy place of TROY.
Persephone	The Queen of the Underworld and wife of HADES.
Perseus	The hero who killed MEDUSA and was the faithful husband of ANDROMEDA.
Phaedra	ARIADNE'S sister and wife of THESEUS. When she fell in love with his son, HIPPOLYTUS, she killed herself.
Phaëthon	The son of APOLLO, whose wish to drive his father's chariot for one day almost led to the end of the world.
Phantasus	Variously, the son or brother of HYPNOS. Phantasus was the God of Dreams of Inanimate Objects.
Phaon	An old boatman to whom APHRODITE gave youth and beauty for ferrying her from Lesbos to Chios.
Philemon	A poor old man who with his wife was blessed by the gods, given a temple to live in, and promised that he would never live alone without her.
Phineus	A prophet whom ZEUS cursed by having HARPIES defile his food whenever he wanted to eat.

Phobos	The God of Fear. He accompanied ARES into battle.
Phoebe	A TITAN who was the first Moon Goddess.
Pholus	A centaur-friend of Heracles (HERCULES).
Pirene	Famous spring in Corinth.
Pittheus	King of Troezen and the father of THESEUS'S mother.
Pluto	The God of the Underworld. (See HADES.)
Plutus	The God of Wealth, a Roman allegorical figure.
Poena	The Roman Goddess of Punishment. The Greeks regarded her as an attendant of NEMESIS.
Pollux	The son of LEDA, who with his brother CASTOR was the Special Protector of Sailors.
Polybus	King of CORINTH, whom OEDIPUS believed was his father.
Polydeuces	Another name for POLLUX.
Polydorus	A son of PRIAM. According to Homer, he was killed by ACHILLES.
Polyidus	A wise seer of Corinth.
Polyxena	HECUBA'S daughter who was killed on ACHILLES' grave.
Pomenis	One of ACTAEON'S hounds; the name means "leader."

Pomona	The first NUMINA. She was later personified and became the Goddess of Gardens and Orchards.
Pontus	The God of the Deep Sea. He was a son of Mother Earth and the father of the Sea God NEREUS.
Poseidon	The God of the Sea, who was CRONUS'S son and ZEUS'S brother.
Priam	King of TROY, during the war against the Greeks.
Priapus	The God of Fertility.
Procne	PHILOMELA'S sister, who avenged her sister's punishment by killing her own son and feeding him to her husband, TEREUS. The gods changed her into a nightingale.
Procris	The niece of PROCNE and PHILOMELA, who was accidentally killed with her husband's javelin.
Procrustes	A man who tied his victims onto an iron bed and cut or stretched them to fit on the bed. THESEUS killed Procrustes in the same manner.
Proetus	The king of ARGOS.
Prometheus	The Titan whose name means "forethought." He sided with ZEUS in his war with the TITANS.
Proserpine	Another name for PERSEPHONE.
Proteus	The god sometimes said to be POSEIDON'S son and sometimes said to be his attendant. Proetus could foretell the future and change his shape, at will.

Psyche — A beautiful maiden who married CUPID and was given immortality.

Pterelas — One of ACTAEON'S hounds; the name means "winged."

Pygmalion — The sculptor who fell in love with his statue of a woman. APHRODITE brought the sculpture to life, as GALATEA, and the two were married.

Pylades — ORESTES' friend and cousin who helped avenge Agamemnon's murder.

Pylos — NESTOR'S home.

Pyramus — The beautiful youth who loved THISBE and killed himself because he thought she was dead. The red fruit of the mulberry is a memorial to the lovers.

Pyrrha — One of two people saved from the Flood that destroyed the world.

Python — A serpent killed by APOLLO.

Remus — One of the twin brothers who founded Rome. As children, they were washed ashore by the Tiber and saved by a she-wolf who fed them her milk. (See ROMULUS.)

Rhea — CRONUS'S sister-queen. She was the mother of ZEUS, POSEIDON, HADES, DEMETER, HERA, and HESTIA.

Rhesus — The TROJANS' Thracian ally, whose horses surpassed all mortal ones.

Romulus — REMUS'S twin brother who helped found Rome. (See REMUS.)

Salmoneus — A man who pretended to be ZEUS. The god struck him down with a lightning bolt.

Sarpedon	The son of ZEUS and EUROPA. He fought with the TROJANS against the Greeks.
Saturn	The Roman name for CRONUS.
Satyrs	Goat-men who were followers of PAN.
Scamander	The name used by mortals for the great river of TROY (called Xanthos by the gods).
Scheria	The country of the Phaeacians in the Odyssey.
Sciron	A man who made those he captured kneel to wash his feet and then would kick them down to the sea. THESEUS threw him over a precipice.
Scorpio	The scorpion, one of the signs of the Zodiac.
Scylla	A sea nymph whom CIRCE changed into a monster with serpents and dogs' heads coming from her body. Scylla destroyed all sailors who passed her.
Scyros	The island where THESEUS died and ACHILLIES disguised himself as a girl.
Selene	The Moon Goddess. Selene was one of ARTEMIS'S three forms.
Selli	The people who made bread from acorns in ZEUS'S sacred grove.
Semele	DIONYSUS'S mother whom ZEUS loved.
Sibyl	A prophetess who guided AENEAS to the Underworld.

Sidero	TYRO'S maid who married her husband and was killed by Tyro's son, PELIAS.
Sileni	Followers of DIONYSUS and PAN, who were part man and part horse.
Silenus	A jovial fat old man who was always drunk. He was said to be PAN'S brother or son.
Simois	One of the rivers of TROY.
Siren	One of the creatures with beautiful voices who lived on an island in the sea and lured sailors to their deaths.
Sirius	The Dog Star in the constellation Canis Major.
Sol	The Roman God of the sun.
Sphinx	The creature shaped like a winged lion with the breast and face of a woman. She beseiged THEBES until OEDIPUS answered her riddle.
Sterope	One of ATLAS'S daughters who was placed in the heavens as a star.
Stricta	One of ACTAEON'S hounds; the name means "spot."
Styx	The river of the unbreakable oath in the Underworld. Anyone who broke such an oath was banished from the council of the gods and denied nectar and ambrosia.
Sylvanus	One of the NUMINA; the Helper of Plowmen and Woodcutters.
Syracuse	The greatest city of Sicily.
Syrinx	A nymph loved by PAN. Her sister nymphs turned her into a tuft of reeds to save her from him, but he made the reeds into a pipe.

Talus	Last of the Bronze race. Talus was made completely of bronze except for one ankle.
Tantalus	ZEUS'S son whom the gods loved. Tantalus hated the gods and served them his son to eat. They discovered his treachery and punished him by putting him in HADES in a pool that drained whenever he tried to drink. They also placed fruit trees above him from which he could never pick fruit.
Tartarus	Another name for the Underworld.
Telamon	The father of AJAX. He was one of the ARGONAUTS.
Telemachus	The son of ODYSSEUS.
Telephus	Heracles' (HERCULES') son. He fought with the Greeks against the TROJANS.
Tempe	A beautiful valley near Mount Olympus.
Tereus	PROCNE'S husband. He was changed into a hawk.
Terminus	A NUMINA who was the Guardian of Boundaries.
Thalia	The MUSE of Comedy. She was also one of the three Graces.
Thamyris	A poet who was struck blind when he challenged the MUSES to a contest.
Thea	A TITAN who married her brother Hyperion and gave birth to the sun.
Thebes	The city founded by Cadmus.
Themis	Right or Divine Justice which sat beside ZEUS in OLYMPUS.

Theridamas   One of ACTAEON'S hounds; the name means "beast-tamer."

Theron   One of ACTAEON'S hounds; the name means "savage-faced."

Theseus   The greatest Athenian hero.

Thespian Lion, The   A lion that ravaged livestock around Mount Cithaeron until Heracles (HERCULES) killed it.

"Ate"—Goddess of Mischief

Thessaly	The site of Mount OLYMPUS in northeastern Greece.
Thestius	A king of Calydon who was the father of LEDA and ALTHEA.
Thetis	The sea nymph who was the mother of ACHILLES.
Thisbe	PYRAMUS'S lover who killed herself after she found him dead. The red fruit of the mulberry tree is a memorial to them.
Thoös	One of ACTAEON'S hounds; the name means "swift."
Thrace	The home of a fierce people in the northeast of Greece.
Tiber	The God of the Tiber River, who instructed AENEAS to go to the site of Rome.
Titan	The elder gods who were huge and strong and ruled over the universe before ZEUS dethroned them.
Tityus	A giant killed by APOLLO and ARTEMIS.
Triton	The Trumpeter of the Sea. He was a son of POSEIDON.
Trivia	Another name for HECATE.
Trojan	An inhabitant of the city of TROY. (See also TROJAN in Chapter 5).
Troy	A wealthy city on the east end of the Mediterranean, where the Trojan War was fought.
Turnus	The king of the Rutulians who was one of LAVINIA'S suitors and consequently battled against AENEAS for her. Turnus lost his life.

Tyche	The Greek name for the Goddess of Fortune.
Tydides	Another name for DIOMEDES.
Tyndaris	The daughter of Tyndareus and LEDA.
Typhoeus	Another name for TYPHON.
Typhon	The monster with a hundred heads whom ZEUS conquered.
Tyro	The woman who bore POSEIDON twin sons, PELIAS and NELEUS.
Ulysses	Another name for ODYSSEUS.
Urania	The MUSE of Astronomy.
Uranis	One of ACTAEON'S hounds; the name means "heavenly one."
Uranus	The father of CRONUS, the TITANS, the CYCLOPS, and the Furies.
Venus	The Roman name for APHRODITE.
Vesper	Another name for HESPER.
Vesta	The Roman name for HESTIA.
Victoria	The Roman name for NIKE.
Virbius	The Roman name for HIPPOLYTUS.
Voluptas	The Roman Goddess of Pleasure.

Vulcan   The Roman name for HEPHAESTUS.

Xanthus   The gods' name for TROY'S great river.

Zephyr   The God of the West Wind.

Zetes   One of the ARGONAUTS.

Zethus   The twin brother of Amphion. Together, they built a wall around THEBES to fortify it.

Zeus   The Supreme God of the Universe.

"Moses"

CHAPTER **7**

Religious Names

All things bright and beautiful,
All creatures great and small,
All things wise and wonderful,
The Lord God made them all.

Cecil Frances Alexander
from *All Things Bright and Beautiful*

This chapter contains names from the world's major religions. Most of the suggestions are from the Judeo-Christian tradition—particularly the Old and New Testaments; but many are derived from Hindu, Buddhist, or Islamic scriptures and related sources.

Religious Names

Aaron	MOSES' brother whose rod became a serpent, when he cast it before Pharaoh. Aaron and his sons became the first priests of the Tabernacle.
Abednego	One of DANIEL'S three friends who survived the fiery furnace.
Abel	The son of ADAM and EVE. Abel's brother, CAIN, murdered him.
Abraham	The founder of the Hebrew people.
Absalom	A son of King DAVID who led a revolt against his father.
Adam	The first man created by God.
Agni	The Hindu fire god.
Ahab	The seventh king of the Northern Kingdom who married JEZEBEL. She persuaded him to abandon the worship of God for BAAL, the pagan deity.
Amalek	Esau's grandson who founded a warlike tribe that fought the Israelites.
Amos	A Hebrew prophet.
Ananias	An early Jewish Christian. When he and his wife lied to God, PETER denounced them, and they died.
Andrew	The brother of PETER who was one of the first disciples of Jesus.
Anna	A Hebrew prophetess who worshiped the infant Jesus.
Annas	The High Priest CAIAPHAS's father-in-law. When Jesus appeared before him after his arrest, Annas sent him to Caiaphas.

Antipas	One of Herod's sons who ruled Galilee and Perea during Jesus' lifetime. Antipas ordered JOHN THE BAPTIST beheaded.
Archelaus	One of Herod's sons who ruled Judea when JOSEPH (2), MARY (see MARY THE VIRGIN), and Jesus returned from Egypt.
Asenath	The wife of JOSEPH (1) who bore him two sons, Manasseh and EPHRAIM.
Baal	A pagan god worshiped in Phoenicia and Canaan whom some of the Israelites began to worship, angering God.
Barabbas	The robber whom PONTIUS PILATE released instead of Jesus.
Barak	The leader of Israel's forces against the Canaanite forces of King Jabin.
Barnabas	An early convert to Christianity who with PAUL preached the Gospel of Jesus.
Bartholomew	One of the Twelve Apostles, also known as NATHANAEL in one of the Gospels.
Bartimaeus	A blind beggar whose faith in Jesus restored his sight.
Bast	The Egyptian Goddess of Matrimony and Feminine Sensuality. Bast was originally represented as a cat.
Beelzebub	A pagan god whom the Philistines worshiped. He is sometimes identified with Satan.
Belshazzar	The Babylonian ruler for whom DANIEL interpreted the significance of the handwriting on the wall.

Religious Names

Benjamin	The youngest of Jacob's and Rachel's twelve sons.
Boaz	RUTH's second husband to whom she bore a son named Obed.
Brahma	The supreme Hindu deity, called Creator of the Worlds.
Buddha (Guatama)	The founder of Buddhism, which holds that suffering is inherent in life but that one can rise beyond it by mental and moral self-purification.
Caiaphas	The High Priest, a friend of the Romans, who tried Jesus and then turned Him over to PONTIUS PILATE.
Cain	The first-born son of ADAM and EVE. He killed his brother, ABEL.
Caleb	MOSES' spy who reported on the Canaanites' strength.
Chilion	NAOMI's and ELIMELECH's son.
Chuza	The husband of JOANNA.
Cleopas	One of the two disciples with whom Jesus spoke on the way to Emmaus after the Resurrection.
Cornelius	A Roman centurion who saw a vision and then was baptized by PETER, thus becoming the first Gentile to convert to Christianity.
Cush	A son of HAM named after the land where his descendants lived.
Cyrus	The founder of the Persian Empire who released the Jews and told them to return to Jerusalem.
Dagon	One of the Philistines' pagan gods.

Dalai Lama	The spiritual leader of the Tibetan and Mongolian branch of Buddhism.
Daniel	Israel's great prophet whom God delivered from the lions' den.
Darius	The Babylonian king who cast DANIEL to the lions because of his great love for God.
David	The boy who slew the giant GOLIATH and went on to become the greatest of Israel's kings. He built the city of Jerusalem.
Deborah	A prophetess who helped BARAK defeat the Canaanites.
Delilah	SAMSON'S love who betrayed him to the Philistines.
Demas	An early Christian who accompanied PAUL during his first Roman imprisonment.
Demetrius	A silversmith who incited a riot against PAUL because the latter's preaching had ruined the man's sale of silver models of the temple of the goddess Diana.
Dinah	A daughter of JACOB and Leah.
Dionysius	An Athenian whom PAUL converted and who became the first bishop of Athens.
Dorcas	Another name for Tabitha, a woman disciple whom PETER raised from the dead.
Drusilla	A daughter of Herod Agrippa I.
Eleazar	One of AARON'S sons who became High Priest after his father's death.

Religious Names

Eli	The priest at Shiloh. Hannah brought her son SAMUEL to him.
Elijah	A great prophet of Israel who opposed AHAB and Queen JEZEBEL by fighting against the worship of the BAAL.
Elimelech	NAOMI's husband and father of RUTH's first husband, Mahlon.
Elisabeth	The mother of JOHN THE BAPTIST and a cousin of Mary (see MARY THE VIRGIN), the mother of Jesus.
Elisha	The prophet who succeeded ELIJAH.
Elkanah	The husband of HANNAH who was the father of the prophet SAMUEL.
Enoch	CAIN's eldest son.
Epaenetus	The first Greek convert to Christianity.
Epaphras	An early Christian friend of PAUL.
Ephraim	JOSEPH's second son. Part of Canaan was named for him.
Erastus	One of PAUL's attendants who went as a missionary into Macedonia.
Esau	ISAAC's eldest son who sold his birthright to his brother JACOB for a bowl of lentils.
Esther	A Hebrew orphan girl who married Ahasuerus (Xerxes), the King of Persia, and consequently was able to save her people from persecution.
Eutychus	A young man who fell from a window while listening to PAUL. The apostle restored his life.

Eve	The first woman created by God.
Ezekiel	A major Hebrew prophet.
Ezra	A Hebrew priest and scholar.
Felix	The Roman procurator who tried PAUL.
Gabriel	The archangel who announced the birth of Christ to the Virgin Mary (see MARY THE VIRGIN) and told her what to name Him.
Gad	The son of JACOB and Zilpah who founded one of the Twelve Tribes of Israel.
Gedaliah	The Hebrew governor appointed by NEBUCHADNEZZAR.
Gehazi	The Prophet ELISHA's servant who was cursed with leprosy for betraying his master.
Gershon	One of the three grandsons of JACOB who accompanied him to Eygpt.
Gideon	One of the great judges of Israel, whom God chose to free the Children of Israel from the threat of the Midianites and other hostile tribes.
Goliath	The giant whom DAVID killed.
Habakkuk	A minor Hebrew prophet.
Hagar	SARAH's handmaid. She was the mother of ISHMAEL, who is regarded as the ancestor of the Arabs.
Haggai	A minor Hebrew prophet.

Religious Names

Ham	One of NOAH'S sons. Ham is considered the ancestor of all black Africans.
Hamutal	The mother of two kings—Jehoahaz and Zedekiah.
Hannah	The mother of SAMUEL, the judge and prophet.
Hanuman	The monkey god in Hindu mythology.
Heman	A musician and dancer and the grandson of the prophet SAMUEL. Heman sang and played in the temple during the reign of King DAVID.
Hephzibah	Wife of King HEZEKIAH. The name means "my delight is in her."
Herodias	Herod Antipas's wife who actually was instrumental in the death of JOHN THE BAPTIST.
Hezekiah	A king of Judah who reclaimed some of his nation's lands from the Philistines.
Hilkiah	A high priest who discovered the lost *Book of the Law*, or *Deuteronomy*.
Hophni	ELI'S son who, with his brother, died in battle, losing the Ark of the Covenant to the Philistines.
Hosea	A minor prophet.
Hur	A Hebrew who stood by MOSES during the battle with AMALEK.
Ichabod	The grandson of ELI.
Indra	The Hindu Rain God, the King of heaven.

Isaac	ABRAHAM's son whom Abraham almost sacrificed to God to prove his faith. Isaac married REBEKAH, and they had two sons, ESAU and JACOB.
Isaiah	Generally regarded as the greatest Hebrew prophet.
Ishmael	Abraham's son by HAGAR, his wife's handmaid. Ishmael founded a great nation of people in Arabia, where the Muslims revere him.
Israel	The name given to JACOB by an angel, which the Twelve Hebrew Tribes later adopted.
Jacob	Son of ISAAC and REBEKAH, who wrestled with the angel of the Lord and consequently was named ISRAEL.
Jambavat	The Hindu King of the Bears.
James	(1) The son of Alphaeus who became one of the Twelve Apostles. (2) The Apostle who was the son of ZEBEDEE and the brother of JOHN.
Jehoshaphat	One of JUDAH's greatest kings, who tried to abolish paganism and who was a great military leader.
Jeremiah	A major Hebrew prophet.
Jesse	King DAVID's father.
Jezebel	The evil queen married to King AHAB. She persecuted the Israelites until chariot horses trampled her to death.
Joanna	One of Jesus' earliest followers.

Religious Names

Job
: A man who suffered a long series of great miseries. His name has become synonymous with patience.

John
: One of the Twelve Apostles. He is considered the author of *Revelations* and the *Gospel of John*.

John the Baptist
: Jesus' forerunner.

Jonah
: The Hebrew prophet who was swallowed by a whale because he did not want to go to Nineveh to preach. He repented and went to Nineveh.

Joseph
: (1) One of JACOB'S and RACHEL'S sons. Joseph's jealous brothers sold him as a slave into Egypt. (2) The husband of Mary (see MARY THE VIRGIN), the mother of Jesus.

Joshua
: An Israelite who after MOSES' death led his people in their first conquests in Canaan.

Judah
: JACOB'S fourth son who founded the largest of the Twelve Tribes of Israel.

Judas Iscariot
: The Apostle who betrayed Jesus to His enemies.

Jude
: The son of Mary (see MARY THE VIRGIN) and JOSEPH, thus believed by some to be a brother of Jesus.

Kama
: The Hindu God of Love.

Kasmir (or Katmir or Kitmir)
: The dog, according to Muslim tradition, that was one of the animals Mohammed admitted to Paradise.

Krishna
: An incarnation of VISHNU.

Lazarus	Jesus' friend and the brother of MARTHA and MARY OF BETHANY. Jesus raised Lazarus from the dead.
Levi	One of JACOB's sons. Levi founded one of the Twelve Tribes of Israel.
Lot	ABRAHAM's nephew whom God saved, along with his family, from the destruction of Sodom.
Lucifer	The light-bearer; the star that brings in the day (the morning star). Originally an archangel, Lucifer led a rebellion, was cast out of heaven, and became identified with the Devil.
Luke	An early Christian who accompanied PAUL on two of his missionary journeys. The third gospel is attributed to Luke.
Lydia	A wealthy woman who was PAUL's first European convert.
Malachi	A prophet of Israel.
Mark	One of the Evangelists. He is considered the author of the *Gospel of Mark*.
Martha	The sister of LAZARUS and MARY OF BETHANY.
Mary Magdalene	A woman who was one of Jesus' devoted followers. She was one of the two women who discovered Jesus' empty tomb.
Mary of Bethany	The sister of MARTHA and LAZARUS, who anointed Jesus in Simon the Leper's house.
Mary the Virgin	The mother of Jesus and wife of JOSEPH.

Matthew	One of the Twelve Apostles whose original name was LEVI. The *Gospel of Matthew* is ascribed to him.
Matthias	The disciple chosen to take the place of JUDAS.
Mecca	The birthplace of MOHAMMED in Saudi Arabia and the Islamic holy city.
Meshach	One of DANIEL'S three companions who survived the fiery furnace.
Methuselah	A Biblical figure who was renowned for his longevity.
Meuzza	MOHAMMED'S beloved cat. She was one of the animals admitted to Islamic Paradise.
Micah	A minor Hebrew prophet.
Miriam	MOSES and AARON's sister who became a prophetess.
Mohammed	The founder of the Islamic religion.
Moses	The Hebrew prophet who led the Israelites out of Egypt and who received the Ten Commandments from God.
Naomi	The mother-in-law of RUTH.
Nathanael	One of the Twelve Apostles, known as BARTHOLOMEW in the first three Gospels.
Nebuchadnezzar	A powerful king of Babylon who invaded Israel several times, carrying its people into bondage and razing Jerusalem and the Holy Temple.

Nicodemus	A Pharisee who defended Jesus at one of His trials, and buried Him after the Crucifixion.
Noah	The builder of the ark who saved himself, his family, and two of each of the world's animals from the Flood.
Obadiah	A minor prophet.
Obed	The grandfather of King DAVID.
Paul	The first Christian missionary who had persecuted Christians until he saw a vision on the road to Damascus.
Peter	The Apostle who as a fisherman had been called SIMON (THE CANAANITE). Jesus changed his name to Peter, meaning "rock."
Philip	One of the Twelve Apostles.
Pontius Pilate	The Roman procurator of Judea who tried and condemned Jesus.
Ra	The Eygptian God of the Sun.
Rachel	The wife of JACOB and mother of his sons, JOSEPH and BENJAMIN.
Rama	The Hindu king who was the son of VISHNU, his incarnation on earth.
Ravan	The Hindu demon king.
Rebekah	The wife of ABRAHAM's son ISAAC and mother of his sons, ESAU and JACOB.
Reuben	JACOB's first son who founded one of the Twelve Tribes of Israel.

Religious Names

Ruth	The young woman whose story is told in the Old Testament *Book of Ruth*. She was the great-grandmother of King DAVID.
Samson	The strongest man in the Bible who received his strength from his long hair. His love, DELILAH, betrayed him.
Samuel	A prophet and judge of Israel who delivered the Israelites at Mizpah from Philistine oppression and who anointed SAUL as the first king of Israel.
Sarah	The wife of ABRAHAM.
Sarama	The great god INDRA'S watchdog and messenger in Hindu mythology.
Sarameyau	SARAMA'S savage twin sons in Hindu mythology, who guided the souls of the dead to their final resting place.
Saraswati	The Hindu Goddess of Speech.
Saul	The first king of Israel.
Seth	The third son of ADAM and EVE.
Shadrach	One of DANIEL'S three companions who survived the fiery furnace.
Sheba (Queen of)	The wealthy queen who visited King SOLOMON.
Shiva	The great Hindu god whose third eye will destroy the world.
Simeon	A son of JACOB and LEAH, who founded one of the Twelve Tribes of Israel.
Simon (the Canaanite)	One of the Twelve Apostles.

Simon of Cyrene	The man who carried the cross for Jesus.
Sita	RAMA's wife, the ideal Hindu woman.
Solomon	King DAVID's son who became the third king of Israel and built the first temple.
Stephen	An early Christian. He was stoned to death for his beliefs, thereby becoming the first Christian martyr.
Thaddaeus	One of the Twelve Apostles. He is also called Jude and Lebbaeus.
Thomas	The Apostle known as "doubting Thomas" because he would not believe in the Resurrection until he saw Jesus' wounds.
Timothy	PAUL's friend and companion.
Titus	PAUL's Greek assistant and companion, who was converted by him.
Tobit's Dog	(1) One of the animals placed in Islamic Paradise. (2) The dog who appears in the *Book of Tobit* in the Apocrypha to the Bible.
Varuna	The Hindu God of the Waters.
Vayu	The Hindu God of the Wind.
Vishnu	The great Hindu god who preserves the three worlds.
Yama	The Hindu God of Death.
Zacharias	A priest who was the father of JOHN THE BAPTIST.

Religious Names

Zebedee — The father of the two apostles JAMES and JOHN.

Zechariah (or Zachariah) — A priest and minor Hebrew prophet whose visions and teachings appear in the Old Testament that bears his name.

Zephaniah — A minor prophet of Israel whose teachings appear in the Old Testament named for him.

Zoroaster — A Persian religious teacher, the founder of the Zoroastrian religion.

CHAPTER 8

Royalty and Titles

I'll call thee Hamlet,
King, father, Royal Dane: Oh, answer me!

William Shakespeare
from *Hamlet*

There is no better way to exalt your pet and show your high esteem than by giving it a prestigious title. Most of the names in this section are royal designations, but quite a few are derived from military or civil terms.

Royalty and Titles

Admiral
Airman
Ambassador
Baron
Baroness
Barrister
Brigadier (General)

Brother
Cadet
Captain
Chancellor
Chief
Coach
Colonel

Commander
Corporal
Counselor
Count
Countess
Czar (Tsar)
Czarina (Tsarina)

Dean
Detective
Director
Doctor
Duchess
Duke
Earl

"Pasha"

Emperor	Lord	Officer	Rey
Empress	Madame	Pasha	Ruler
Ensign	Mademoiselle	Patriarch	Seaman
General	Maestro	Pharaoh	Secretary
Gladiator	Majesty	Preacher	Senator
Governor	Major	Premier	Senior
Highness	Master	President	Señor
Inspector	Matriarch	Prime Minister	Señorita
Judge	Mayor	Prince	Sergeant
Kaiser	Midshipman	Princess	Shah
Khan	Minister	Private	Sheik
King	Miss	Queen/Queenie	Shogun
Knight	Mister	Rabbi	Sir
Lady	Mistress	Representative	Sister
Leader	Monsieur	Reverend	Squire
Lieutenant	Ms.	Rex	Teacher

"McDuff"

CHAPTER 9

Foreign Words and Names

A man who is ignorant of foreign languages is ignorant of his own.

Johann von Goethe

If you have a flair for the exotic or simply want to impress your friends with your linguistic skills, then the names in this chapter will intrigue you (and possibly prompt you to open a foreign language dictionary!). Your best choice is a pleasant sounding word, preferably one you can pronounce correctly, and one with a translation that appropriately fits your pet. For instance, be careful not to embarrass yourself and your black cat by naming him Amarillo, the Spanish word for "yellow"!

Foreign Words and Names

Abogado	Spanish for "lawyer."
Agape	Greek for word meaning "love."
Allegre	Spanish for "happy."
Aloha	Hawaiian word for "hello" or "goodbye."
Amarillo(a)	Spanish for "yellow." Use Amarillo for a male and Amarilla for a female.
Amigo(a)	Spanish word meaning "friend." Use Amigo for a male and Amiga for a female.
Amore	Italian for "love."
Astra	Latin for "star."
Azul	Spanish for "blue."
Beau/Belle	French for "handsome/beautiful" (male/female).
Bébé	French for "baby."
Beeren	German for "berries."
Bello(a)	Italian for "pretty."
Bianca Pinjarra	Some of the crown jewels of England.
Bianco(a)	Italian for "white." Use Bianco for a male and Bianca for a female.
Bier	German word for "beer."

Bijou	French for "jewel."
Blanco(a)	Spanish for "white." Use Blanco for a male and Blanca for a female.
Blanquito(a)	Spanish for "little white one." Use Blanquito for a male and Blanquita for a female.
Bleu/Bleue	French for "blue" (male/female).
Bobae	Korean for "heirloom."
Boca	Spanish for "mouth."
Bonito(a)	Spanish for "pretty." Use Bonito for a male and Bonita for a female.
Canela	Spanish for "cinnamon."
Caro/Cara	Italian for "dear" (male/female). Gaelic for "friend."
Celia	"Little heavenly one."
Chansu	Japanese for "chance."
Chat	French for "cat."
Chatool	Hebrew for "cat."
Chico	Spanish for "young man."
Chien	French for "dog."
Chiquita	Spanish for "little girl."
Cinco	Spanish for "five."

Foreign Words and Names

Coeur	French for "heart."
Concha	Spanish for "shell."
Deja Vu	French for "already seen."
Diablo	Spanish for "devil."
Diez	Spanish for "ten."
Dolce	Italian for "sweet."
Dono	Italian for "gift."
Dos	Spanish for "two."
Faeden	Gaelic for "golden."
Faux Pas	French for "a social blunder."
Felice	Italian for "happy."
Feliz	Spanish for "happy."
Feo	Spanish for "ugly."
Fiesta	Spanish for "party."
Flavo	Italian for "fair or blonde."
Fraulein	German for "young woman."
Freida	A German name for a female.

Frieden	German for "peace."
Frijol	Spanish for "bean."
Fritz	A German name for a male.
Gato(a)	Spanish for "cat." Use *Gato* for a male and *Gata* for a female.
Gigio	Italian for "cricket."
Greta	A German name for a female.
Gretchen	A German name for a female.
Gretel	A German name for a female.
Gris	Spanish for "gray."
Hans	A German name for a male.
Heidi	A German name for a female.
Heinrich	A German name for a male; it translates as "Henry."
Hombre	Spanish for "man."
Hummel	A German name for a male.
Ilsa	A German name for a female.
José	A Spanish name for a male.
Kannika	"Jasmine-like blossom" in Japanese.

Foreign Words and Names

Katarina (Katrina)	A Russian name for a female.
Keseff	Hebrew for "silver."
Klein	German for "small."
Kochka	Russian for "cat."
Kui	Hawaiian for "roar."
Kut	The Egyptian name for the male cat.
Kutta	The Egyptian name for the female cat.
Laddie	Scottish for "young man."
Lassie	Scottish for "young woman."
Lieb	German for "dear."
Liesel	A German name for a female.
Linda	Spanish for "pretty."
Luna	Spanish for "moon."
Madame	French for "Mrs. or Madam."
Mademoiselle	French for "Miss."
Mar	Spanish for "sea."
Marta	A German name for a female.
McCloud	A Scottish name.

"Sushi"

Foreign Words and Names

McDuff	A Scottish name.
McMurphy	A Scottish name.
McTavish	A Scottish name.
Mesa	Spanish for "table."
Mi	Spanish for "my."
Misha	A Russian name for a male.
Monique	A French name for a female.
Monsieur	French for "Mister."
Muñeca	Spanish for "doll."
Natasha	A Russian name for a female.
Nicole	A French name for a female.
Nikko	Japanese for "cat."
Nueve	Spanish for "nine."
Ocho	Spanish for "eight."
Octavia/n	A Latin name for a female/male.
Omar	A Middle Eastern name.
Oso(a)	Spanish for "bear." Use Oso for a male and Osa for a female.
Paco	A Spanish name for a male.

Pancho	A Spanish name for a male.
Pepe	A Spanish name for a male.
Perro(a)	Spanish for "dog." Use Perro for a male and Perra for a female.
Poco	Spanish for "little."
Quatro	Spanish for "four."
Renée	A French name.
Rio	Spanish for "river."
Rojo(a)	Spanish for "red." Use Rojo for a male and Roja for a female.
Rosita	A Spanish name for a female.
Sasha	A Russian name.
Sayonara	Japanese for "goodbye."
Schnell	German for "fast" or "quick."
Schotzie	A German name.
Seis	Spanish for "six."
Señor	Spanish for "Mister."
Señorita	Spanish for "Miss."
Siete	Spanish for "seven."
Simba	African for "lion."

Foreign Words and Names

Som Phong	Tai word meaning "like one's ancestors."
Suki	A Japanese name.
Summa	Latin for "the most."
Sushi	Japanese for "raw fish."
Taiko	Japanese for "boss."
Tanya	A Russian name for a female.
Tasha	A Russian name for a female. (Short for Natasha.)
Tia	Spanish for "aunt."
Tigre(a)	Spanish for "tiger." Use Tigre for a male and Tigra for a female.
Tio	Spanish for "uncle."
Toro	Spanish for "bull."
Toutou	French for "doggie."
Tres	Spanish for "three."
Trinka	A German name for a female. (Short for Katrinka.)
Uno	Spanish for "one."
Vaquero	Spanish for "cowboy."
Wolfgang	A German name for a male.

"Faux Pas"

"Puss in Boots"

CHAPTER 10

Literature and Art

Ghastly grim and ancient Raven wandering
from the nightly shore—
Tell me what thy lordly name is on the
Night's Plutonian shore!
Quoth the raven, "Nevermore."

Edgar Allan Poe
from *The Raven*

Some of the most memorable animals are those that appear in literature and art. This chapter includes many of those animals, particularly dogs and cats, as well as a few famous human literary and artistic characters.

Adonis	Title character in the Shakespearean narrative poem *Venus and Adonis*.
Agatha Christie	The famous twentieth-century mystery writer.
Aladdin	The boy hero who releases a magic genie by rubbing a magic lamp in *The Thousand and One Nights*.
Alidoro	A mastiff in Carlos Collodi's (Lorenzini) *Pinocchio* (1883). Pinocchio saved Alidoro from drowning; in return Alidoro rescued the puppet from being fried like a fish when coated with flour.
Ann	One of the bluetick hounds of the pair Ann and DAN in the book *Where the Red Fern Grows* by Wilson Rawls.
Antony (Mark)	(Marcus Antonius, 83?–30 B.C.) Triumvir in Rome with Octavian and Marcus Aemilius Lepidus after the murder of Julius Caesar. Also a character in the Shakespearean plays *Antony and Cleopatra* and *Julius Caesar*.
Appollinaris	A cat that belonged to Mark Twain.
Ariel	A delicate spirit in the Shakespearean play *The Tempest*.
Aristophanes	A Greek comedy writer during the last half of the fifth and first half of the fourth centuries B.C. He refers to the myths in his works.
Ashley	The master of Twelve Oaks in Margaret Mitchell's classic novel *Gone With the Wind* (1936).
Aurora	A character from Jimmy Buffett's *Tales from Margaritaville*.

Banshee	A female spirit in Gaelic folklore whose appearance or wailing warns a family of the approaching death of one of its members.
Barge	In *The Fireside Book of Dog Stories* (1943), James Thurber tells of Barge, a watchdog who lived with a family in Columbus, Ohio. Barge took to drinking and neglected his duties until he came home one day and found that burglars had broken into his house. In despair and shame, Barge jumped out of a window and killed himself.
Baron	A dachshund in the book *Park Avenue Vet*, written by Louis J. Camuti.
Basket	Gertrude Stein's two dogs of the same name. They are described in works that Stein wrote in France during the period of the German occupation (1940–1945).
Ben	A dog described by Maxwell Knight, in *My Pet Friends*.
Beowulf	The hero of the Anglo-Saxon epic poem *Beowulf*.
Bevis	A large hound that was a prominent figure in Sir Walter Scott's novel *Woodstock* and was characterized after his own Scottish deerhound.
Big Red	The $7,000 Irish setter in Jim Kjelgaard's *Big Red* (1945). Big Red ruined his chances to be a show dog when he injured himself fighting a wolverine and a bear, thereby saving his master Danny Pickett.
Bilbo Baggins	One of the hobbits in J. R. Tolkien's novels.
Bion	An Alexandrian pastoral poet who wrote of the myths, around 250 B.C.
Blackie	A black spaniel that was Ernest Hemingway's companion for twelve years.

Literature and Art

Blanche | One of the dogs that does not appear on stage but is mentioned in Act 3, Scene 6 of SHAKESPEARE'S play *King Lear* (1608).

Boatswain | Lord Byron's Newfoundland and the subject of a moving epitaph by the well-known poet.

Bodger | The old bull terrier in Sheila Burnford's *The Incredible Journey* (1961). Bodger was one of the three pets who faced tremendous hardships while traveling home through the Canadian wilderness.

Bond (James) | The main character and British spy in the popular Ian Fleming fictional series.

Boring Alice | A character from Jimmy Buffett's *Tales from Margaritaville*.

Brownie | The female Irish setter owned by T. H. White, the author of *The Once and Future King* (1958). White described his love for Brownie in his letters to David Garnett.

Buck | The large, powerful, mix-breed dog in Jack London's *The Call of the Wild*. Stolen from his home in California to be sold as a sled dog in Alaska, Buck was "beaten but not broken." He eventually joined a pack of wolves who signaled their acceptance of Buck by sniffing noses and howling at the moon.

Bull's-eye | The white shaggy mutt in Charles Dickens's *Oliver Twist* (1839). Bull's-eye belonged to the murderer, Bill Sikes, and had as unpleasant a disposition as his owner.

Bunyan (Paul) | The mythical lumberjack hero of the American West.

Cadpig	The smallest and prettiest of Pongo's fifteen puppies in Dodie Smith's *The Hundred and One Dalmatians* (1956). Cadpig's favorite pastime is watching television.
Caesar (Julius)	The powerful Roman political and military leader (100–44 B.C.) who was eventually murdered by Brutus.
Caliban	A character in the Shakespearean play *The Tempest*.
Catarina	A large tortoiseshell cat that belonged to Edgar Allan Poe and his wife Virginia. Catarina would lie on Virginia to keep her warm when Virginia was bedridden.
Catfish	Columnist Lewis Grizzard's dog who, as Grizzard reports in his column, liked to drink out of the toilet.
Charley	The large French poodle that accompanied John Steinbeck on his trip through the United States in the 1960s. Steinbeck recalls their adventures in *Travels with Charley* in which Charley is described as being his ambassador when meeting strange people.
Charlotte	A spider, the title character in *Charlotte's Web* by E. B. White. She saves the life of WILBUR the pig.
Chaucer (Geoffrey)	The greatest English poet of the Middle Ages who is best known for his classic, *The Canterbury Tales*.
Cheshire Cat, The	The famous grinning cat whom Alice encounters during her journey in *Alice's Adventures in Wonderland* (1865) by Lewis Carroll. (See also *Cheshire Cat* in Chapter 11.)

Cinderella | The girl who marries Prince Charming in the well-known fairy tale *Cinderella*.

Clarissa | A dog in James Thurber's *How to Name a Dog*.

Clifford | Title character of Norman Bridwell's children's book, *Clifford the Big Red Dog*.

Columbine | A stock character in early Italian comedy and pantomime. Columbine was the daughter of Pantaloon and the sweetheart of HARLEQUIN.

Cotton-Tail | The brother of FLOPSY and MOPSY. These three were the "good little bunnies [who] went down to the lane to gather blackberries," from Beatrix Potter's *The Tale of Peter Rabbit*.

Cujo | The canine title character of a Stephen KING novel.

Da Vinci (Leonardo) | The renowned Italian painter, artist, sculptor, and architect (1452–1519).

Damn Spot | From SHAKESPEARE'S *Macbeth* (published in 1623), in which Lady Macbeth proclaimed: "Out, out, Damn spot" while walking through the castle distraught over the blood on her garment after killing King Duncan.

Dan | Half of the pair ANN and Dan in the book *Where the Red Fern Grows*.

Dante (Alighieri) | One of the greatest medieval poets. Dante's major literary work was *The Divine Comedy*.

Dash | A mongrel dog that belonged to writer Charles Lamb. Dash had once belonged to poet Thomas Hood. Lamb wrote about Dash's "crazy" behavior, which included the ability to stand on his hind legs.

Dash — Dashiell Hammett (1894–1961), an American crime novelist whose works include *The Maltese Falcon* and *The Thin Man*.

Dickens (Charles) — One of the most popular English novelists who criticized the wealthy and corrupt in nineteenth-century England.

Digit — A gorilla in the book *Gorillas in the Mist* by Diane Fosse (1983). He got his name from the fourth and fifth digits of his hand, which were webbed.

Dinah — Alice's cat, who was left behind when Alice fell down the rabbit-hole in Lewis Carroll's *Alice's Adventures in Wonderland* (1865).

Diogenes — The brutish dog that adored his owner, Florence Dombey, in Charles Dickens's *Dombey and Son* (1848).

Don Juan — One of the most famous literary figures in medieval legends. Don Juan has appeared in the works of Byron, Shaw, Moliere, and Mozart.

Dr. Watson — Sherlock Holmes's companion and the narrator of Sir Arthur Conan Doyle's (1859–1930) mystery books.

Duke — Penrod Schofield's dog. A scraggly, but faithful, companion in Booth Tarkington's *Penrod* (1914). (See also *Duke* in Chapter 5.)

El Dorado — The fictitious kingdom of untold wealth on the Amazon River for which Spanish and English explorers searched.

Emerson (Ralph Waldo) — American poet, essayist, and lecturer (1803–1882).

Euripides	A Greek tragic poet of the fifth century B.C., who wrote plays based on myths.
Feathers	Carl van Vechten's cat, whose behavior he discussed in *The Tiger in the House* (1920).
Flicka	The title character in a novel about a horse, entitled *My Friend Flicka*.
Flopsy	One of the "good little bunnies" in Beatrix Potter's stories. (See COTTON-TAIL.)
Flossy	English writer Anne Bronte's fat little black-and-white spaniel.
Flush	Elizabeth Barrett Browning's red cocker spaniel. Elizabeth was holding Flush when she met Robert in Hodgson's Bookshop in 1846.
Fortitude	One of two lions whose statues guard the Fifth Avenue entrance to the main building of the New York Public Library. (See PATIENCE.)
Foss	Edward Lear's beloved tomcat for whom he created "The Heraldic Blazon of Foss the Cat," published in *Nonsense Songs, Stories, Botany and Alphabets*.
Frost (Robert)	One of America's greatest twentieth-century poets and winner of the Pulitzer Prize in 1924, 1931, 1937, and 1943 (1874–1965).
Fu Manchu	The villain in Sax Rohmer novels.
Gatsby (Jay)	A racketeer of the 1920s in F. Scott Fitzgerald's classic novel *The Great Gatsby* (1925).

Gipsy	The cat who left home to become an alley cat in Booth Tarkington's *Penrod and Sam*.
Goldilocks	The little girl in the children's fairy tale *The Three Bears*.
Grendel	An anthropomorphic monster who ravaged Herot for twelve years and was killed by BEOWULF in the novel *Beowulf*.
Grimalkin	The demon spirit in the form of a cat mentioned by the First Witch in SHAKESPEARE'S *Macbeth* (1605).
Guinevere	KING ARTHUR'S wife in the stories of King Arthur and the Round Table.
Gulliver	Title character in Jonathan Swift's *Gulliver's Travels* (1726).
Hamlet	Title character of a Shakespearean play, published in 1603.
Harlequin	A clown in early Italian comedy and pantomime. Harlequin's tight-fitting costume has alternating patches of contrasting colors.
Hank the Cowdog	Title character of a children's book series by John R. Erikson.
Heidi	The heroine of *Heidi* by Johanna Spyri (1827–1901).
Hemingway (Ernest)	American novelist (1899–1961), 1954 winner of the Nobel Prize. Wrote *The Sun Also Rises*, *A Farewell to Arms*, *The Old Man and The Sea*, and *The Snows of Kilimanjaro*, among others.
Herodotus	The first historian of Europe. He refers to the myths in his works.
Hinse	The cat that belonged to the poet and novelist Sir Walter Scott of Edinburgh (1771–1832).

Holden	The main character in J. D. Salinger's novel *Catcher in the Rye* (1951).
Homer	The blind poet who wrote of the Greek myths in *The Iliad* and *The Odyssey*.
Horatio	Character in the Shakespearean play *Hamlet*.
Hound of the Baskervilles, The	The ghostly black hound that dwelt on the moors of Dartmoor and terrorized the Baskerville family in Sir Arthur Conan Doyle's *The Hound of the Baskervilles* (1902).
Jack	Title character in the Mother Goose nursery rhyme "Jack and Jill."
Jeannie	A Scotty that appears in *Thurber's Dogs* (1955).
Jennie	The discontented Sealyham terrier that became the star of the World Mother Goose Theatre in Maurice Sendak's *Higglety Pigglety Pop! or There Must Be More to Life* (1967).
Jill	Title character in the Mother Goose nursery rhyme "Jack and Jill."
Jip	(1) Dora Spenlow's small black spaniel who liked to walk on the dinner table in Charles Dickens's *David Copperfield* (1850). (2) The dog with an acute sense of smell that helped save a man stranded on an island in Hugh Lofting's *The Story of Doctor Dolittle* (1920).
Juliet	One of the star-crossed lovers in SHAKESPEARE'S *Romeo and Juliet* (1594–95).
Keeper	Emily Brontë's mastiff. When his mistress died, Keeper followed the coffin in the funeral procession and slept for nights at the door of her empty room.

Kiche	The she-wolf that whelped in Jack London's *White Fang* (1906).
King (Stephen)	A contemporary author of horror books, including *Carrie*, *The Shining*, *Pet Sematary*, and *The Dead Zone*.
King Arthur	The legendary king of the Britons who restored order and peace in his kingdom. King Arthur's story is told in various literary works.
Kipling (Rudyard)	English poet, short story writer, and novelist (1865–1936); wrote *The Light That Failed* and *The Jungle Book*, as well as the well-known poem *Gunga Din*, among other works.
Lad	The thoroughbred collie who accomplished amazing deeds in Albert Payson Terhune's *Lad: A Dog* (1919). Terhune based Lad on his own collie, Sunnybank Lad.
Lady Godiva	The wife of Loefric, Earl of Mercia and Lord of Coventry. She rode naked through the town to get her husband to lower heavy taxes on the people (c.1040–1080).
Lancelot	Sir Lancelot du Lac, the best of KING ARTHUR'S knights, who loved Arthur's wife GUINEVERE in the stories of King Arthur and the Round Table.
Lassie	The collie in Eric Knight's pre-World War II short story "Lassie Come Home" (1938), who has since become a symbol of loyalty and dignity.
Lion of Lucerne, The (Lowendenkmal)	A statue of a dying lion erected in Lucerne's Glacier Garden to commemorate the Swiss Guards who were killed defending Louis XVI during the French Revolution.

Lobo

The "King of Currumpaw," leader of a pack of wolves that attacked cattle in New Mexico. Ernest Thompson Seton wrote of his attempts to capture Lobo in *Wild Animals I Have Known* (1898). Seton finally succeeded by luring the wolf with the dead body of his mate, Blanca.

Longfellow
(Henry Wadsworth)

The most popular and accomplished poet of the nineteenth century (1807–1882).

Lucian

A second-century A.D. Greek writer who satirized the gods.

Lysander

Character in the Shakespearean play *A Midsummer Night's Dream*.

Macavity

The ginger cat that mysteriously disappears whenever anything turns up missing in "Macavity: the Mystery Cat" from *Old Possum's Book of Practical Cats* (1939) by T. S. Eliot.

Macbeth

Title character of a Shakespearean play.

Marcellus

Character in the Shakespearean play *Hamlet*.

Max

A dachshund that is mentioned by Matthew Arnold in the elegy "Poor Matthias" (1882). See also MORITZ.

Merlin the
Magician

The legendary sorcerer who advised Arthur to establish the Round Table.

Merrylegs

Jupe's performing circus dog in Charles Dickens's *Hard Times* (1854) who disappeared with his owner, only to return to the circus alone, lame, and almost blind.

Michelangelo | The immensely talented Florentine painter, sculptor, architect, and poet (1475–1564) who was known for, among other things, his painting of the ceiling of the Sistine Chapel in Rome.

Minnaloushe | A black cat that is the subject of three verses in William Butler Yeats's *The Cat and the Moon* (1919).

Miss Muffet | The girl frightened by a spider in the popular nursery rhyme.

Mistigris | Madame Vauquer's cat in Honore de Balzac's *Le Père Goriot* (1835).

Mittens | The kitten who laughed so hard she fell off the wall in Beatrix Potter's *The Tale of Tom Kitten*.

Mona Lisa | Leonardo Da Vinci's famous painting of the woman with the mysterious smile.

Monsieur Tibault | The cat that conducted a symphony orchestra with his tail in Stephen Vincent Benét's *The King of the Cats* (1929).

Moppet | One of the two kittens that "trod upon their pinafores and fell on their noses," in Beatrix Potter's *The Tale of Tom Kitten*.

Mopsy | One of the "good little bunnies" in Beatrix Potter's stories. (See COTTON-TAIL.)

Moritz | From *Max and Moritz*, the German classic by Wilhelm Busch. The names designate a pair of mischief-makers.

Morris | The famous finicky, striped tomcat of 9-Lives Cat Food commercials whose biography was written by Mary Daniels in 1974.

Mouschi	A cat that belonged to Ann Frank as described in *Diary of a Young Girl*.
Mozart (Wolfgang Amadeus)	Austrian composer who began to write music at the age of five. He wrote more than forty symphonies and twenty-two operas, among other great musical works.
Muggs	(1) The ferocious airedale in James Thurber's "The Dog That Bit People" from *My Life and Hard Times* (1933). (2) One of James Thurber's dogs included in his book, *Thurber's Dogs* (1955).
Music	The female greyhound described by William Wordsworth in the poem, "Incident Characteristic of a Favorite Dog" (1805). Music, who belonged to Mrs. Wordsworth's brother, tried desperately to save her friend Dart who had fallen through the ice on a lake. As she was breaking away the ice with her paws, Wordsworth described the scene: ". . . For herself she hath no fears/Him alone she sees and hears."
Mutt	An amusing, black-and-white mongrel in Farley Mowat's *The Dog Who Wouldn't Be* (1957).
Nana	The Newfoundland dog that is the Darling children's nurse in J. M. Barrie's *Peter Pan* (1904).
Nero	Jane Welsh Carlyle's white terrier, part Maltese and part mongrel, who one day jumped from the library window, knocking himself senseless. Virginia Woolf relates the incident, claiming that perhaps the dog was attempting suicide, in *Flush* (1933).
Nox	The big black retriever whose behavior helped Father Brown solve Colonel Druce's murder in G. K. Chesterton's "The Oracle of the Dog" from *The Incredulity of Father Brown* (1926).

Octavian (Augustus) Julius Caesar's great-nephew (63 B.C.–A.D. 14).

Old Bob | The gray collie that was an award-winning sheepherder in *Bob, Son of Battle* (1898) by Alfred Ollivant.

Old Yeller | The rugged, stray yellow-gold dog who was adopted in Fred Gipson's *Old Yeller*, a novel about the Texas hill country in the frontier days of the 1860s. Old Yeller's name had a double meaning: the color of his hair coat and the yelling sounds he made.

Oliver (Twist) | The orphan in Charles Dickens's novel *Oliver Twist* (1837–39).

Othello | Title character of a Shakespearean play published in 1622.

Ovid | A Latin narrative poet who retold almost all of the stories of classical mythology.

Oz | From the novel *The Wonderful Wizard of Oz* (1900) by L. Frank Baum about Dorothy, a Kansas farm girl who was swept away by a tornado to the land of Oz.

Patience | One of two lions whose statues guard the Fifth Avenue entrance to the main building of the New York Public Library. (See FORTITUDE.)

Pepper | The names of three of Dandie Dinmont's six terriers (the other three were named MUSTARD) in Sir Walter Scott's *Guy Mannering* (1815).

Peter Rabbit | The mischievous little rabbit in Beatrix Potter's *The Tale of Peter Rabbit*. When Peter was hiding under a flower pot, he sneezed and was discovered by Mr. McGregor.

Phoebe | Holden's sister in J. D. Salinger's novel *Catcher in the Rye* (1951).

Picasso (Pablo)	Famous Spanish artist and sculptor (1881–1973); the leading figure in modern art.
Pindar	Greece's greatest lyric poet who alludes to the myths in all his poems.
Pinocchio	The puppet whose nose grew when he lied in *Pinocchio* (1883) by Carlos Collodi (Lorenzini).
Professor Moriarity	The arch enemy of Sherlock Holmes in Sir Arthur Conan Doyle's (1859–1930) mystery books.
Prynne (Hester)	The main character in Nathaniel Hawthorne's 1850 novel *The Scarlet Letter*.
Puck	A character in the Shakespearean play *A Midsummer Night's Dream*.
Puss in Boots	The clever cat that was the sole inheritance a poor boy received from his father. The cat, who asked only for a pair of boots, tricked an ogre by challenging him to turn himself into a mouse. The cat ate the ogre, and his master took over the ogre's lands and castle.
Pyramus	A character in the Shakespearean play *A Midsummer Night's Dream*.
Rab	The powerful dog in Dr. John Brown's *Rab and His Friends* that kept a vigil at the bedside of his owner Ailie during her illness and subsequent death.
Raksha	The Mother Wolf that raised Mowgli in Rudyard Kipling's *The Jungle Book* (1894).
Rembrandt	A Dutch Baroque painter (1606–1669) whose works, including *The Night Watch*, have become treasured masterpieces.

Remus (Uncle)	The narrator of a series of stories by Joel Chandler Harris (1848–1908). Uncle Remus was a former slave who became a beloved family servant and who entertains a young boy by telling him animal stories.
Rhett	Rhett Butler, the irreverent Southerner who becomes Scarlett's third husband in Margaret Mitchell's *Gone With the Wind* (1936).
Rikki-Tikki-Tavi	The title character in RUDYARD KIPLING'S short story about a mongoose that fights cobras.
Rinnie	Nickname for *Rin Tin Tin*. (See Chapter 11.)
Romeo	One of the star-crossed lovers in SHAKESPEARE'S *Romeo and Juliet* (1594–95).
Rum Tum Tugger	A fictional cat in *Old Possum's Book of Practical Cats* by T. S. Eliot (1939).
Salinger (J. D.)	An American author (b. 1919), best known for his novel *Catcher in the Rye* (1951).
Savage Sam	OLD YELLER'S son in Fred Gipson's novel *Savage Sam* (1962).
Scarlett	The heroine of Margaret Mitchell's *Gone With the Wind* (1936).
Schuster	See SIMON.
Selima	Horace Walpole's tabby cat who was immortalized in a poem by Thomas Gray. Selima drowned in a goldfish bowl white trying to catch a fish. (Indeed, "curiosity killed the cat!")

Sergeant Murphy — The brown dog that is a motorcycle-riding police officer in Richard Scarry's picture books.

Shakespeare (William) — (1564–1616) The English playwright who is known as history's greatest dramatist and the best English-language poet.

Shep — Shep, a collie that took care of a flock of sheep in New York City's Central Park, is described in an early twentieth-century story.

Sherlock Holmes — The famous detective in Sir Arthur Conan Doyle's (1859–1930) books.

Shimbleshanks — One of the cats in *Old Possum's Book of Practical Cats* by T. S. Eliot (1939).

Simon — Co-founder of Simon & SCHUSTER, a major New York publisher.

Simpkin — The tailor's cat in Beatrix Potter's *The Tailor of Gloucester* (1903).

Sinbad (the Sailor) — The sailor whose adventures include battling monsters in *The Arabian Nights*.

Sneakers — A cat about whom Margaret Wise Brown wrote in her *Seven Stories About a Cat Named Sneakers*.

Sophocles — A Greek playwright who wrote about the myths.

Sounder — The sharecropper's faithful dog with the resonant voice in William H. Armstrong's *Sounder* (1969).

Sour Mash — One of Mark Twain's several feline pets.

Sputnik	The first man-made satellite launched by the Soviet Union on October 4, 1957.
Stumpy	The big brown dog in Beatrix Potter's *The Tale of Little Pig Robinson* (1930).
Sweetheart	A dog referred to in Act 3, Scene 6 of SHAKESPEARE'S *King Lear* (1608).
Tabitha (Tabby)	A Siamese cat in *One Kitten Too Many* by Bianco Bradbury. Tabitha was called Tabby for short.
Tabitha Twitchit	The mother cat that was a shrewd businesswoman in Beatrix Potter's books.
Tailspin	The cat that was born on the moon in *Space Cat* by Ruthven Todd.
Tao	The male Siamese cat in *The Incredible Journey* (1961) by Sheila Burnford.
Tara	The O'Hara family's plantation in Margaret Mitchell's classic novel, *Gone With the Wind* (1936).
Tessa	A dog that belonged to author James Thurber.
Theocritus	An Alexandrian pastoral poet who wrote of the gods.
Tiger	The cat that played with KEEPER, the dog, in the household of Emily and Charlotte Brontë. (See also TIGER in Chapter 5.)
Tigger	The bouncy tiger in A. A. Milne's *The House at Pooh Corner* (1928).
Tinkerbell	The tiny fairy in *Peter Pan* (1904) by J. M. Barrie.

Titian	One of the greatest painters of the Renaissance. This Italian master lived c. 1488–1576.
Toby	(1) A puppet dog in the Punch and Judy shows. (2) The ugly part spaniel who assists Sherlock Holmes and Dr. Watson in Sir Arthur Conan Doyle's *The Sign of Four* (1890).
Tom Kitten	The naughty kitten in Beatrix Potter's *The Tale of Tom Kitten*, who was so fat his buttons burst off his clothes. He later lost his clothes, which were found by some ducks who wore them.
Tom Quartz	A kitten that President Theodore Roosevelt named for the fictional cat Tom Quartz in Mark Twain's book *Roughing It* (1872).
Toto	The dog that journeys with Dorothy in L. Frank Baum's *The Wonderful Wizard of Oz* (1900).
Toulouse-Lautrec (Henri de)	A leading postimpressionist artist whose works depicted the sordid late nineteenth-century Parisian society.
Tray	The dog in Thomas Campbell's poem "The Harper."
Van Gogh (Vincent)	The Dutch postimpressionist painter (1853–1890) whose works convey a wide spectrum of emotions.
Venus	Title character in the Shakespearean play *Venus and Adonis*.
Virgil	A Roman poet who wrote of the myths.
Wilbur	The pig in *Charlotte's Web* by E. B. White.

William

(1) Charles Dickens' (1812–1870) dear white cat, which he renamed Williamina when she had kittens. (2) The egotistical cat obsessed with his own name in James Thurber's "The Cat in the Lifeboat" from *Further Fables for Our Time* (1956).

Winnie-the-Pooh

The opinionated but delightful hero of A. A. Milne's stories about a teddy bear and his friends.

Wolf

The dog that accompanied Rip Van Winkle on the day that he fell asleep for twenty years (from Washington Irving's story of Rip Van Winkle).

Zoroaster

One of Mark Twain's several cats.

CHAPTER 11

Screen and Television

The play's the thing . . . !

William Shakespeare
from *Hamlet*

Who's the star of your household? Perhaps it's "Tonto," "Dracula," "Lassie," or maybe "Morris." Take your pick. But be careful; sometimes animals assume the characteristics of their namesakes. (Beware of "Pepe Le Pew.")

Abbott (Bud)	The sly con man in the Abbott and COSTELLO comedy team of the 1930s, '40s, and '50s.
Al Pacino	Academy Award winner, Best Actor, for his role in the movie, *Scent of a Woman* (1992).
Al	TIM's "assistant" in the 1999s television series *Home Improvement*.
Alice Kramden	The wife of RALPH KRAMDEN, played by JACKIE GLEASON, in the 1950s television series *The Honeymooners*.
Amos	The character played by Alvin Childress on the television show *Amos 'n Andy*.
Andy	The character played by Spencer Williams on the television show *Amos 'n Andy*.
Angelina Jolie	Academy Award winner, Best Supporting Actress, for her role in the movie *Girl, Interrupted* (1999).
Anna Magnani	Academy Award winner, Best Actress, for her role in the movie, *The Rose Tattoo* (1955).
Anne Bancroft	Academy Award winner, Best Actress, for her role in the movie, *The Miracle Worker* (1962).
Anthony Hopkins	Academy Award winner, Best Actor, for his role in the movie, *The Silence of the Lambs* (1991).
Apollo	One of the two doberman pinschers owned by Robbin Masters on the television series *Magnum P.I.* (See ZEUS.)

Archie Bunker	The bigoted character played by Carroll O'Connor in the television series *All in the Family*.
Arnold	The pet pig in the television series *Green Acres* starring Eddie Albert and Eva Gabor.
Art Carney	Academy Award winner, Best Actor, for his role in the movie, *Harry and Tonto* (1974). Friend of RALPH KRAMDEN, played by JACKIE GLEASON, in the 1950s television series *The Honeymooners*.
Arthur	The drunken millionaire played by DUDLEY MOORE in the movie *Arthur*.
Asta	The wirehaired fox terrier in the television series *The Thin Man*. The Humane Association gave Asta two Patsy Awards for exceptional performance.
Audrey Hepburn	Academy Award winner, Best Actress, for her role in the movie, *Roman Holiday* (1953).
B. J. Hunnicut	HAWKEYE'S buddy on the television series *M*A*S*H*.
Bagheera	The black panther in the Walt Disney movie *The Jungle Book* (1966).
Bailey	A character in the television series *Party of Five*.
Baloo	The bear in Walt Disney's movie *The Jungle Book* (1966).
Bam Bam	BARNEY and Betty Rubble's son in Hanna-Barbera's animated television cartoon *The Flintstones*.
Bambi	The fawn in Walt Disney's animated movie *Bambi* (1942).

Barbra Streisand	Academy Award winner, Best Actress, for her role in the movie *Funny Girl* (1968).
Barnabas Collins	The vampire in the television series *Dark Shadows*.
Barnaby Jones	The private eye played by Buddy Ebsen in the television series *Barnaby Jones*.
Barney (Rubble)	The best friend of Fred Flintstone in Hanna-Barbera's animated television cartoon *The Flintstones*.
Barney Fife	The bungling deputy (1960–1965) in the television series *The Andy Griffith Show*.
Bart Maverick	One of the brothers, played by Jack Kelly, living in the frontier west in the television series *Maverick*.
Bashful	One of the Seven Dwarfs in the Walt Disney movie *Snow White and the Seven Dwarfs* (1937).
Batman	Batman first appeared in *Detective Comics* in May 1939. In the spring of 1940, *Batman Comics* evolved. The Mutual Radio Network also featured the voices of Batman and ROBIN during the 1940s. The ABC television series ran from 1966 until 1968. The first movie *Batman* (1989) featured Michael Keaton in the title role. The second movie, *Batman Returns* (1992), also starred Michael Keaton. The third movie, *Batman Forever* (1995), starred Val Kilmer.
Beaver (Cleaver)	The hapless younger son of the Cleavers in the television series *Leave It to Beaver*.
Beeswax	A cat in the 1989 Tom Selleck film *Her Alibi*.

Ben Kingsley	Academy Award winner, Best Actor, for his role in the movie, *Gandhi* (1982).
Benji	The shaggy mutt who became a star, appearing in *Benji* (1974), *For the Love of Benji* (1977), and *Oh Heavenly Dog* (1980).
Bert	One of the muppet characters in the television series *Sesame Street*. (See ERNIE and OSCAR THE GROUCH.)
Bette Davis	Academy Award winner, Best Actress, for her roles in the movies *Dangerous* (1935), and *Jezebel* (1938).
Bing Crosby	Academy Award winner, Best Actor, for his role in the movie, *Going My Way* (1944).
Bloop Bloop	The extraterrestrial creature from the television series *Lost in Space* (1965–1968).
Bogart (or Bogey)	Humphrey Bogart, the famous actor, who starred in numerous films.
Bojangles (Bill Robinson)	A dancer and entertainer (1878–1949), appeared in SHIRLEY TEMPLE movies.
Boo-Boo Kitty	SHIRLEY'S stuffed cat in the television series *Laverne and Shirley*.
Bosley	The man who acts as an intermediary between the elusive Charlie and his female detectives in the television series *Charlie's Angels*.
Brady	The name of the family in the television series *The Brady Bunch*.
Brando (Marlon)	One of the most famous American actors after World War II. Brando won Academy Awards for his performances in *On the Waterfront* (1954) and *The Godfather* (1972).

Bret Maverick	One of the brothers, played by James Garner, living in the frontier west in the television series *Maverick*.
Brewster	The baseball player, played by Richard Pryor, who inherits a fortune in the movie *Brewster's Millions*.
Broderick Crawford	Academy Award winner, Best Actor, for his role in the movie, *All the King's Men* (1949).
Brubaker	The prison inspector played by Robert Redford in the movie *Brubaker*.
Bubba	The friend of FORREST GUMP in the Academy Award-winning (1994) movie *Forrest Gump* starring TOM HANKS.
Bud	A character played by Charlie Sheen in the movie *Wall Street*.
Buffy	The little blonde-haired girl in the television series *Family Affair*.
Bullet	Roy Rogers' German shepherd who debuted in the movie *Spoilers of the Plains* (1951) and later appeared on the *Roy Rogers Show*.
Burt Lancaster	Academy Award winner, Best Actor, for his role in the movie, *Elmer Gantry* (1960).
Burt Reynolds	Actor who has starred in a variety of movies in the 1960s, '70s, and '80s.
Butch Cassidy	The western outlaw played by PAUL NEWMAN in the 1969 movie *Butch Cassidy and the Sundance Kid*. (See SUNDANCE KID.)
Butkus	ROCKY'S dog in the original movie *Rocky*.

Car Face	The sinister gang leader "Junkyard Dog" in the 1989 animated cartoon *All Dogs Go to Heaven*.
Carrie Bradshaw	Columnist played by Sarah Jessica Parker on the television series *Sex and the City*.
Carson Daly	Host of *Last Call with Carson Daly* and the MTV television series *Total Request Live*.
Cat Ballou	The main character of the 1965 movie *Cat Ballou*.
Chandler Bing	Businessman played by Matthew Perry in the television series *Friends*.
Charlie Chaplin	One of the most famous actors in motion picture history. Chaplin is best remembered for his roles in silent films.
Charlie	The lead character in the animated movie *All Dogs Go To Heaven* (1989).
Charlotte York	An art gallery curator played by Kristin Davis on *Sex and the City*.
Charlton Heston	Academy Award winner, Best Actress, for his role in the movie, *Ben Hur* (1959).
Cher	Academy Award winner, Best Actress, for her role in the movie, *Moonstruck* (1987).
Cheshire Cat	The grinning cat who fades away except for his grin. Created by Lewis Carroll, the Cheshire Cat appeared in Walt Disney's animated movie *Alice in Wonderland* (1951). (See also *Cheshire Cat* in Chapter 10.)
Chewbacca (or Chewy)	The 100-year-old "Wookie" in the movie *Star Wars* (1977) and its sequels.

Chinook	The white German shepherd who costarred with Kirby Grant in a series of movies about a Mountie and his dog (1949–1954). Chinook later played White Shadow in the *Mickey Mouse Club's* Corky and White Shadow serial.
Cinderella	The fairy-tale heroine who marries Prince Charming in Walt Disney's animated movie *Cinderella*.
Clarabell	The puppet clown in the 1950s television series *Howdy Doody*.
Clark Gable	The popular American film star (1901–1960) once called "The King," best known for his role as Rhett Butler in the 1939 movie *Gone With the Wind*.
Clark Griswold	The lead character in the National Lampoon *Vacation* movie series starring Chevy Chase.
Claudette Colbert	Academy Award winner, Best Actress, for her role in the movie, *It Happened One Night* (1934).
Claw	The one-eyed foe of Combo in *Combo the White Lion*.
Cleo	The glum-faced basset hound who commented on the characters and events in the 1950s television show *The People's Choice*.
Cliff Robertson	Academy Award winner, Best Actor, for his role in the movie, *Charly* (1968).
Costello (Lou)	The rotund victimized member of the ABBOTT and Costello comedy team.
Cuba Gooding, Jr.	Academy Award winner, Best Supporting Actor, for his role in the movie *Jerry Maguire*.

Curly

(1) One of the characters in the movie series *The Three Stooges*. (2) The tough trail boss played by Jack Palance in the movie *City Slickers*.

Daniel Day-Lewis

Academy Award winner, Best Actor, for his role in the movie, *My Left Foot* (1989).

Daphne Moon

Former housekeeper played by Jane Leeves on the television series *Frasier*.

Darth Vader

The commander of the forces of evil in the movie *Star Wars* (1977) and its sequels.

David Niven

Academy Award winner, Best Actor, for his role in the movie, *Separate Tables* (1958).

Diane Keaton

Academy Award winner, Best Actress, for her role in the movie, *Annie Hall* (1977).

Dickinson (Angie)

An actress who has starred in both television and movie roles, including the television series *Police Woman*.

Dobie Gillis

A romantically inclined teenage boy in the television series *The Many Loves of Dobie Gillis*. Dobie also appeared in the movie *The Affairs of Dobie Gillis* (1953).

Doc

One of the Seven Dwarfs in Walt Disney's animated movie *Snow White and the Seven Dwarfs* (1937).

Dolly (Parton)

The country western singer, song writer, and actress (*Nine to Five*). She appeared in her own television variety show *Dolly*. She also opened her own theme park, Dollywood, in Tennessee in 1986.

Dopey	One of the Seven Dwarfs in Walt Disney's animated movie *Snow White and the Seven Dwarfs* (1937).
Dracula	The vampire created by the novelist Bram Stoker, who first appeared in the 1931 movie *Dracula, The Un-Dead*.
Duchess	A Parisian cat in Walt Disney's animated movie, *The Aristocats* (1970). Duchess has a romance with O'Malley, the alley cat.
Dudley (Moore)	The contemporary comedian and movie star.
Duke	An airedale owned by famous Western actor John Wayne. The dog's name inspired Wayne's nickname, "The Duke."
Dustin Hoffman	Academy Award winner, Best Actor, for his roles in the movies, *Kramer vs. Kramer* (1979), and *Rain Man* (1988).
Eddie	The dog who is Martin Crane's constant companion on *Frasier*.
E. T.	The extraterrestrial being in Steven Spielberg's movie *E.T.*
Elaine	A character on the television series *Seinfeld* played by Julia Louis-Dreyfus.
Elizabeth Taylor	Academy Award winner, Best Actress, for her roles in the movies, *Butterfield 8* (1960), and *Who's Afraid of Virginia Wolf?* (1965).
Elsa	The lioness whose story is told in the movie *Born Free* and in a television series. Elsa's story was first told in a book by Joy Adamson.
Ernest Borgnine	Academy Award winner, Best Actor, for his role in the movie, *Marty* (1954).

Ernie	One of the muppet characters in the television series *Sesame Street*. (See BERT and OSCAR THE GROUCH.)
Ethel Mertz	The wife of Fred Mertz in the *I Love Lucy* television series.
Ewok	One of the furry, teddy bearlike creatures in the movie *The Return of the Jedi*.
F. Murray Abraham	Academy Award winner, Best Actor, for his role in the movie, *Amadeus* (1984).
Fantasia	A 1940 Walt Disney feature film.
Farrah (Fawcett)	The actress who first became famous in the television series *Charlie's Angels*.
Faye Dunaway	Academy Award winner, Best Actress, for her role in the movie, *Network* (1976).
Felix	The fussy character played by Jack Lemmon in the movie *The Odd Couple* and by Tony Randall in the television series.
Festus	The old deputy in the television series *Gunsmoke*.
Fez	Foreign exchange student played by Wilmer Valderrama on the television series *That 70's Show*.
Figaro	The kitten who kissed a fish in Walt Disney's animated film, *Pinocchio* (1940).
Flower	The skunk in the animated feature movie *Bambi* (1942).

Fonzie — The nickname of the cool high school dropout, played by Henry Winkler, in the television series *Happy Days*.

Forrest Gump — The character in the Academy Award-movie starring TOM HANKS.

Frances McDormand — Academy Award winner, Best Actress, for her role in the movie *Fargo* (1996).

Frank Sinatra — Academy Award winner, Best Supporting Actor, for his role in the movie, *From Here to Eternity* (1953).

Frasier Crane — Psychologist played by Kelsey Grammer on the television series *Frasier*.

Fredric March — Academy Award winner, Best Actor, for his roles in the movies, *Dr. Jekyll and Mr. Hyde* (1932), and *The Best Years of Our Lives* (1946).

Freeway — The dog in the television series *Hart to Hart*. The Harts found him on the freeway.

Frodo — A hobbit played by Elijah Wood in the movie trilogy *The Lord of the Rings*.

Gary Cooper — Academy Award winner, Best Actor, for his roles in the movies, *Sergeant York* (1941), and *High Noon* (1952).

Gene Hackman — Academy Award winner, Best Actor, for his role in the movie, *The French Connection* (1971).

Geoffrey Rush — Academy Award winner, Best Actor, for his role in the movie *Shine* (1996).

George	Jerry's neurotic friend in the television series *Seinfeld* played by Jason Alexander.
George Arliss	Academy Award winner, Best Actor, for his role in the movie, *Disraeli* (1930).
George Banks	The lead character played by Steve Martin in the movie *Father of the Bride*.
George Burns	A popular comedian (1896–1996); husband of GRACIE ALLEN.
George C. Scott	Academy Award winner, Best Actor, for his role in the movie, *Patton* (1970).
Geraldine Page	Academy Award winner, Best Actress, for her role in the movie, *The Trip to Bountiful* (1985).
Ginger Rogers	Academy Award winner, Best Actress, for her role in the movie, *Kitty Foyle* (1940).
Glenda Jackson	Academy Award winner, Best Actress, for her roles in the movies, *Women in Love* (1970), and *A Touch of Class* (1973).
Glenn Close	Winner of the Tony Award for Best Leading Actress in the musical *Sunset Boulevard*; well-known screen star (*Fatal Attraction, The Big Chill*).
Gomer Pyle	A character in the television series *Gomer Pyle, USMC*.
Goofy	The not-so-bright, black hound who first appeared in Walt Disney's animated MICKEY MOUSE cartoons.

Goose	The call sign of a pilot in the movie *Top Gun*.
Gordon Gecco	The character played by MICHAEL DOUGLAS in the movie *Wall Street*.
Grace Kelly	Academy Award winner, Best Actress, for her role in the movie, *The Country Girl* (1954).
Gracie Allen	A popular comedienne; wife of GEORGE BURNS.
Greer Garson	Academy Award winner, Best Actress, for the movie, *Mrs. Miniver* (1942).
Gregory Peck	Academy Award winner, Best Actor, for his role in the movie, *To Kill a Mockingbird* (1962).
Grumpy	One of the Seven Dwarfs in Walt Disney's animated movie *Snow White and the Seven Dwarfs* (1937).
Grunt	The dog in the movie *Flashdance*.
Gwyneth Paltrow	Academy Award winner, Best Actress, for her role in the movie *Shakespeare in Love* (1998).
Happy	One of the Seven Dwarfs in Walt Disney's animated movie *Snow White and the Seven Dwarfs* (1937).
Hardy (Oliver)	The comedian who co-starred with his partner, LAUREL, in numerous movies.
Harriet (Hilliard Nelson)	The wife of OZZIE in the television series *The Adventures of Ozzie and Harriet* (1952–1966).

Harrison Ford	The actor who played Hans Solo in the *Star Wars* movie series. He also played Indiana Jones in *Raiders of the Lost Ark* and its sequels.
Hawkeye	The irreverent doctor played by Alan Alda in the classic television series *M*A*S*H*.
Hazel (Burke)	The family maid played by Shirley Booth in the television series *Hazel*.
Helen Hayes	Academy Award winner, Best Actress, for her role in the movie, *The Sin of Madelon Claudet* (1931).
Helen Hunt	Academy Award winner, Best Actress, for her role in the movie *As Good As It Gets* (1997).
Henry Fonda	Academy Award winner, Best Actor, for his role in the movie, *On Golden Pond* (1981).
Herbie	"The Love Bug," a Volkswagen, who is the hero in several movies.
Higgins	The dog in the television series *Petticoat Junction* (1963–1970). This was movie star BENJI'S first acting role.
Hilary Swank	Academy Award winner, Best Actress, for her role in the movie *Boys Don't Cry* (1999).
Holly Hunter	Academy Award winner, Best Actress, for her role in the movie, *The Piano* (1993).
Hooch	The large, ugly dog in the movie *Turner and Hooch* (1989).
Huckleberry Hound	The hero of the first all-animated television series, *Huckleberry Hound*, created by Hanna-Barbera Productions in 1958.

Humphrey Bogart	Academy Award winner, Best Actor, for his role in the movie, *The African Queen* (1951).
Ice Man	The call sign of a pilot played by Val Kilmer in the movie *Top Gun*.
Igor	Dr. Frankenstein's assistant in a series of movies about Frankenstein's monster.
Indiana Jones	The swashbuckling hero of *Raiders of the Lost Ark* (and a series of movies that followed in the 1980s), starring HARRISON FORD.
Ingrid Bergman	Academy Award winner, Best Actress, for her roles in the movies, *Gaslight* (1944), and *Anastasia* (1956).
J. R. (Ewing)	The ruthless Texas oilman in the television series *Dallas*.
Jack Lemmon	Academy Award winner, Best Actor, for his role in the movie, *Save the Tiger* (1973).
Jack Nicholson	Academy Award winner, Best Actor, for his role in the movie, *One Flew Over the Cuckoo's Nest* (1975).
Jackie Gleason	Actor and entertainer best known for his role as RALPH KRAMDEN in the 1950s television series *The Honeymooners*.
James Cagney	Academy Award winner, Best Actor, for his role in the movie, *Yankee Doodle Dandy* (1942).
James Stewart	Academy Award winner, Best Actor, for his role in the movie, *The Philadelphia Story* (1940).
Jane Fonda	Academy Award winner, Best Actress, for her roles in the movies, *Klute* (1971), and *Coming Home* (1978).

Jane Wyman	Academy Award winner, Best Actress, for her role in the movie, *Johnny Belinda* (1948).
Janet Gaynor	Academy Award winner, Best Actress, for her role in the movie, *Seventh Heaven* (1927).
Jay Leno	The host of *The Tonight Show*.
Jedi	A warrior and protector of The Empire in the movies *Star Wars, Return of the Jedi*, and *The Empire Strikes Back*.
Jennifer Jones	Academy Award winner, Best Actress, for her role in the movie, *The Song of Bernadette* (1943).
Jeremy Irons	Academy Award winner, Best Actor, for his role in the movie, *Reversal of Fortune* (1990).
Jerry	The famous mouse who, with his partner, the cat TOM, has appeared in numerous MGM, and later Hanna-Barbera, animated cartoons.
Jessica Lange	Academy Award winner, Best Actress, for her role in the movie, *Blue Sky* (1994).
Jessica Tandy	Academy Award winner, Best Actress, for her role in the movie, *Driving Miss Daisy* (1989).
Jessica	The part played by Angela Lansbury in the popular, long-running television series *Murder She Wrote*.
Jill	TIM'S wife and character in the television series *Home Improvement*.
Joan Crawford	Academy Award winner, Best Actress, for her role in the movie, *Mildred Pierce* (1945).

Joan Fontaine	Academy Award winner, Best Actress, for her role in the movie, *Suspicion* (1941).
Joanne Woodward	Academy Award winner, Best Actress, for her role in the movie, *The Three Faces of Eve* (1957).
Jodie Foster	Academy Award winner, Best Actress, for her roles in the movies, *The Accused* (1988), and *The Silence of the Lambs* (1991).
Joey Tribbiani	Struggling actor played by Matt LeBlanc on *Friends*.
John Becker	Physician played by Ted Danson on the television series *Becker*.
John Wayne	The famous actor (1907–1979) best known for his portrayals of tough American Western Frontier characters and war heroes. He won an Academy Award in 1969 for *True Grit*.
Jon Voight	Academy Award winner, Best Actor, for his role in the movie, *Coming Home* (1978).
Joker	The sinister character of *Batman* fame played by Cesar Romero in the television series and by Jack Nicholson in the 1989 movie. (See BATMAN.)
Jose Ferrer	Academy Award winner, Best Actor, for his role in the movie, *Cyrano de Bergerac* (1950).
Judy Holliday	Academy Award winner, Best Actress, for her role in the movie, *Born Yesterday* (1950).
Julie Andrews	Academy Award winner, Best Actress, for her role in the movie, *Mary Poppins* (1964).

Julie Christie — Academy Award winner, Best Actress, for her role in the movie, *Darling* (1965).

Katherine Hepburn — Academy Award winner, Best Actress, for her roles in the movies, *Morning Glory* (1932), *Guess Who's Coming to Dinner?* (1967), *The Lion in Winter* (1968), and *On Golden Pond* (1981).

Kathie Lee — Former co-host of the television talk show *Regis and Kathie Lee*.

Kathy Bates — Academy Award winner, Best Actress, for her role in the movie, *Misery* (1990).

Kevin Spacey — Academy Award winner, Best Actor, for his role in the movie, *American Beauty* (1999).

Kiara — Lioness in the Walt Disney animated movie *The Lion King: Simba's Pride*.

Kimba — The lead character in the 1960s Japanese created television cartoon *Kimba, the White Lion*.

King Kong — Title character of the famous movie about an enormous gorilla (1933).

Kingfish — George Stevens's title on the television series *Amos 'n Andy*.

Kit — The name of the cat in the television series *Charmed*.

Kramer — Jerry's eccentric next-door neighbor in the television series *Seinfeld* played by Michael Richards.

Kukla, Fran & Ollie — The three puppets from the television show *Kukla, Fran, and Ollie*.

Kunta Kinte	The African man captured by slave traders and shipped to America in the television mini-series *Roots* (1977).
Lady	The pretty female cocker spaniel who charmed TRAMP, a disreputable mutt, in Walt Disney Productions' *Lady and the Tramp*.
Larry	One of the characters in the movies series *The Three Stooges*.
Lassie	The collie heroine of the movie *Lassie Come Home* (1943), based on a novel by Eric Knight. This Lassie, followed by many generations of descendants, starred in seven movie sequels, "The Lassie Radio Show," and the *Lassie* television series.
Laurel (Stan)	The slapstick comedian who co-starred with his partner, HARDY, in numerous movies.
Laurence Olivier	Academy Award winner, Best Actor, for his role in the movie, *Hamlet* (1948).
Laverne	Title character, played by Penny Marshall in the 1970s television series *Laverne and Shirley*.
Lee Marvin	Academy Award winner, Best Actor, for his role in the movie, *Cat Ballou* (1965).
Leo	The Metro-Goldwyn-Mayer (MGM) trademark—a lion that appeared on screen in hundreds of movies.
Lionel Barrymore	Academy Award winner, Best Actor, for his role in the movie, *Free Soul* (1930).
Little Dan	A redbone hunting hound in the novel *Where the Red Fern Grows*.

Little Orphan Annie	The little girl created in a comic strip of the same name by Harold Gray in 1924. Little Orphan Annie has appeared in several movies, the first in 1932.
Liza Minnelli	Academy Award winner, Best Actress, for her role in the movie, *Cabaret* (1972).
Lone Ranger	The masked hero of the television series *The Lone Ranger*.
Loretta Young	Academy Award winner, Best Actress, for her role in the movie, *The Farmer's Daughter* (1947).
Louise Fletcher	Academy Award winner, Best Actress, for her role in the movie, *One Flew Over the Cuckoo's Nest* (1975).
Lucy Ricardo	RICKY RICARDO'S wife and star of the 1950s *I Love Lucy* television series starring Lucille Ball.
Luise Rainer	Academy Award winner, Best Actress, for her role in the movie, *The Good Earth* (1937).
Luke Skywalker	The hero of the movie *Stars Wars* (1977) and its sequels.
MacGyver	The title character of a television series.
Maggie Smith	Academy Award winner, Best Actress, for her role in the movie, *The Prime of Miss Jean Brodie* (1969).
Magnum (Thomas)	The private investigator played by Tom Selleck in the television series *Magnum, P.I.*
Marilyn Monroe	Famous celebrity and personality known for her blonde hair and voluptuousness.

Screen and Television

Marlon Brando	Academy Award winner, Best Actor, for his roles in the movies, *On the Waterfront* (1954), and *The Godfather* (1972).
Martin Crane	Frasier's father played by John Mahoney on *Frasier*.
Mary Pickford	Academy Award winner, Best Actress, for her role in the movie, *Coquette* (1928).
Matt Groening	Creator of *The Simpsons* and *Futurama*.
Maverick	The pilot call sign of the lead character played by Tom Cruise in the movie *Top Gun*. Also title of a television series starring James Garner.
Maximilian Schell	Academy Award winner, Best Actor, for his role in the movie, *Judgment at Nuremberg* (1961).
Maynard (G. Krebs)	DOBIE GILLIS's beatnik buddy in the television series *The Many Loves of Dobie Gillis*.
McCloud	The cowboy detective in the television series *McCloud*.
Meatball	A mixed-breed dog who appeared in *Black Sheep Squadron*, a television series with Robert Conrad.
Meathead	ARCHIE BUNKER's derogatory name for his son-in-law in the television series *All in the Family*.
Mel Gibson	Actor and star of numerous movies including *Mad Max*, the *Lethal Weapon* series, and *Braveheart*, which he also directed.
Meryl Streep	Academy Award winner, Best Actress, for her role in the movie, *Sophie's Choice* (1982).

Mia (Farrow)	An actress who has appeared in a variety of movies, including several by Woody Allen.
Michael Douglas	Academy Award winner, Best Actor, for his role in the movie, *Wall Street* (1987).
Mickey Mouse	The world famous star of numerous Walt Disney animated cartoons and movies, and of *The Mickey Mouse Club* television show.
Mickey Rooney	The movie actor known for his movies with Judy Garland in the 1930s and '40s, his Andy Hardy movies, and his part in *National Velvet* (1944).
Mike Judge	Creator of the television series *Beavis and Butthead* and the television series *King of the Hill*.
Milo	Title character in the movie *Milo and Otis*.
Minnie Mouse	Animated cartoon star; MICKEY MOUSE'S female counterpart.
Miranda Hobbes	Lawyer played by Cynthia Nixon on *Sex and the City*.
Miss Ellie	J. R. EWING'S mother in the television series *Dallas*.
Miss Kitty	The owner of Dodge City's bar in the television series *Gunsmoke*.
Miss Piggy	The outrageous leading lady of television's *The Muppet Show* and of *The Muppet Movie* (1979).
Moe	One of the characters in *The Three Stooges*.
Monica Geller	Chef played by Courteney Cox on *Friends*.

Morris	The famous cat that appeared in commercials for 9-Lives Cat Food. Morris also appeared in the movie *Shamus* (1973), and received the first Patsy Award for an animal in commercials.
Mr. T	The impressively large actor who appeared in the television series *The A-Team* and with SYLVESTER STALLONE in one of the sequels to the movie *Rocky*.
Mufasa	Simba's father, a lion in the Walt Disney animated movie *The Lion King*.
Munchkin	One of a group of little people visited by Dorothy in the cinema classic, *The Wizard of Oz*.
Nala	Lioness in the Walt Disney animated movie *The Lion King*.
Navin	The character played by Steve Martin in the movie *The Jerk*.
Neil	The alcoholic St. Bernard from the television series *Topper*.
Newman	Postman played by Wayne Knight on *Seinfeld*.
Niles Crane, Dr.	Frasier's brother, played by David Hyde Pierce, on *Frasier*.
Nina Banks	Played by Diane Keaton, co-star and wife of character George Banks in the movie *Father of the Bride*.
007	The code number for the British spy James Bond, the hero of a series of movies based on novels by Ian Fleming.
Old Dan	A redbone hunting hound from the novel *Where the Red Fern Grows*.

Old Yeller	The rugged, stray yellow-gold dog who was adopted in the movie *Old Yeller*, based on Fred Gipson's book *Old Yeller*. (See also *Old Yeller* in Chapter 10.)
Olivia de Havilland	Academy Award winner, Best Actress, for her roles in the movies, *To Each His Own* (1946), and *The Heiress* (1949).
Omar (Sharif)	The Middle Eastern actor who appeared in numerous movies.
Opie	The boy who portrayed the young son of Andy Griffith in the television series *The Andy Griffith Show*.
Oprah Winfrey	Television talk show hostess and personality.
Oscar	The sloppy character played by Walter Matthau in the movie *The Odd Couple* and by Jack Klugman in the television series.
Oscar the Grouch	One of the muppet characters in the television series *Sesame Street*. (See BERT and ERNIE.)
Otis	Title character in the movie *Milo and Otis*.
Otto	CHARLIE'S buddy in the 1989 musical cartoon *All Dogs Go To Heaven*.
Ozzie (Nelson)	Main character and husband of HARRIET on the television series *The Adventures of Ozzie and Harriet*.
Patricia Neal	Academy Award winner, Best Actress, for her role in the movie, *Hud* (1963).
Paul Lucas	Academy Award winner, Best Actor, for his role in the movie, *Watch on the Rhine* (1943).

Paul Newman	Academy Award winner, Best Actor, for his role in the movie, *The Color of Money* (1986).
Paul Scofield	Academy Award winner, Best Actor, for his role in the movie, *A Man for All Seasons* (1966).
Pebbles	Fred and Wilma Flintstone's daughter in Hanna-Barbera's animated television cartoon *The Flintstones*.
Pegleg Pete	The villainous bulldog with a wooden leg who appeared with MICKEY MOUSE in the Walt Disney films, *Steamboat Willie* (1928) and *Gallopin' Gaucho* (1929).
Pepe Le Pew	The French skunk who appears in several Warner Brothers' animated cartoons.
Percy	The dog in Disney's animated movie *Pocahontas*.
Pete the Pup	The American pit bull terrier with a black circle around one eye and a patch over the other, who appeared in more than eighty episodes of Hal Roach's *Our Gang* comedies.
Peter Pan	The principal character in a play by J. M. Barrie about a boy who didn't want to grow up. Subsequently, he was recreated in the Walt Disney animated movie *Peter Pan*.
Phoebe Buffay	Bubbly blonde played by Lisa Kudrow on *Friends*.
Pluto	Walt Disney's lovable animated hound who appears with MICKEY MOUSE in many of his cartoons.
Pocahontas	Title character in Disney's 1995 animated movie about the Native American Indian maiden who fell in love with Captain John Smith.

Popeye — The sailor who derives his strength from eating spinach. Popeye appeared first in comic strips, and later in animated cartoons and movies.

Potsie — Richie Cunningham's friend in the television series *Happy Days*.

Princess Leia — The heroine of the movie *Stars Wars* (1977) and its sequels.

Pumbaa — A warthog who befriends Simba in *The Lion King*.

Pyewacket — The cat in the film *Bell, Book, and Candle*.

Quincy — Title character in the television series starring Jack Klugman who played a medical examiner.

Rachel Green — Prissy character played by Jennifer Aniston on *Friends*.

Radar — The bespectacled corporal with E.S.P. in the television series *M*A*S*H*.

Rafiki — The wise baboon in the Walt Disney animated movie *The Lion King*.

Rags — Carter's dog in the television series *Spin City*.

Ralph Kramden — The high-strung bus driver played by JACKIE GLEASON in the television series *The Honeymooners*.

Rambo — The character played by SYLVESTER STALLONE in the movie *First Blood* and its sequels.

Ray Barone — Character played by Ray Romano in the television series *Everybody Loves Raymond*.

Ray Milland	Academy Award winner, Best Actor, for his role in the movie, *The Lost Weekend* (1945).
Regis	Half of the host team of the television talk show *Live with Regis and Kelly*.
Rex Harrison	Academy Award winner, Best Actor, for his role in the movie, *My Fair Lady* (1964).
Rhubarb	The striped cat who played the lead role in the 1951 movie version of H. Allen Smith's *Rhubarb* (1946). Rhubarb won a Patsy Award for his performance, and then played Minerva in television's *Our Miss Brooks*. In 1962, Rhubarb won another Patsy as Cat in *Breakfast at Tiffany's*.
Richard Dreyfuss	Academy Award winner, Best Actor, for his role in the movie, *The Goodbye Girl* (1977).
Ricky Ricardo	Lucy's husband and band leader played by Desi Arnaz in the popular television series *I Love Lucy*.
Rin Tin Tin	The German shepherd who after his first film, *Where the North Begins* (1923), appeared in more than forty movies in nine years. His offspring, all given the same name, appeared in subsequent movies and in the television series, *The Adventures of Rin Tin Tin*.
Robert Barone	Ray's brother, played by Brad Garrett, on *Everybody Loves Raymond*.
Robert De Niro	Academy Award winner, Best Actor, for his role in the movie, *Raging Bull* (1980).
Robert Donat	Academy Award winner, Best Actor, for his role in the movie, *Goodbye Mr. Chips* (1939).

Robert Duvall	Academy Award winner, Best Actor, for his role in the movie, *Tender Mercies* (1983).
Roberto Benigni	Academy Award winner, Best Actor, for his role in the movie *Life is Beautiful* (1998).
Robin	The younger half of the BATMAN and Robin combination known as "The Dynamic Duo."
Rochester (Van Jones)	Jack Benny's valet, played by Eddie Anderson.
Rockford	The private detective played by James Garner on the television series *The Rockford Files*.
Rocky	The boxer played by SYLVESTER STALLONE in the movie *Rocky* and its sequels.
Rod Steiger	Academy Award winner, Best Actor, for his role in the movie, *In the Heat of the Night* (1967).
Ronald Colman	Academy Award winner, Best Actor, for his role in the movie, *A Double Life* (1947).
Ross Geller	Palentologist played by David Schwimmer on *Friends*.
Roz Doyle	The on-air radio producer played by Peri Gilpin on *Frasier*.
Russell Crowe	Academy Award winner, Best Actor, for his role in *Gladiator* (2000).
Sally Field	Academy Award winner, Best Actress, for her roles in the movies *Norma Rae* (1979), and *Places in the Heart* (1984).

Samantha Jones	Publicist played by Kim Cattrall on *Sex and the City*.
Sapphire	The wife of George "Kingfish" Stevens in the television series *Amos 'n Andy*. (See KINGFISH.)
Scar	Uncle and foe of Simba in the animated movie *The Lion King*.
Scarlett (O'Hara)	The heroine, played by Vivien Leigh, of the classic movie *Gone With the Wind* (1939), based on the book by Margaret Mitchell.
Scraps	The white mongrel with a brown spot over one eye, who costarred with CHARLIE CHAPLIN in *A Dog's Life* (1918). Scraps went on to star in fifty more films.
Seinfeld (Jerry)	Entertainer and star of the popular television series *Seinfeld*.
Sheena	The "Queen of the Jungle" played by Irish McCalla in both the movie and the television series.
Shirley Booth	Academy Award winner, Best Actress, for her role in the movie *Come Back Little Sheba* (1952).
Shirley MacLaine	Academy Award winner, Best Actress, for her role in the movie *Terms of Endearment* (1983).
Shirley Temple	The most popular child actress of the 1930s, best remembered for her dimples and blonde curly hair.
Shirley	Title character played by Cindy Williams in the television series *Laverne and Shirley*.
Shogun	The Japanese warrior in the television movie *Shogun*.

Sidney Poitier	Academy Award winner, Best Actor, for his role in the movie, *Lillies of the Field* (1963).
Simba	The lead character in the 1994 Walt Disney animated movie *The Lion King*.
Sir Alec Guinness	Academy Award winner, Best Actor, for his role in the movie, *The Bridge Over the River Kwai* (1957).
Sissy Spacek	Academy Award winner, Best Actress, for her role in the movie, *Coal Miner's Daughter* (1980).
Sleepy	One of the Seven Dwarfs in Walt Disney's animated movie *Snow White and the Seven Dwarfs* (1937).
Sly	The nickname for actor SYLVESTER STALLONE.
Sneezy	One of the Seven Dwarfs in Walt Disney's animated movie *Snow White and the Seven Dwarfs* (1937).
Snow White	The fairy tale heroine of Walt Disney's animated movie *Snow White and the Seven Dwarfs* (1937).
Solo	The puniest female pup in an African wild dog pack in Hugo van Lawick's television film *The Wild Dogs of Africa*.
Sophia Loren	Academy Award winner, Best Actress, for her role in the movie, *Two Women* (1961).
Spanky	The fat little boy in the television series *The Little Rascals*.
Spencer Tracy	Academy Award winner, Best Actor, for his roles in the movies, *Captains Courageous* (1937), and *Boys Town* (1938).

Spock	The half Vulcan, half human commander of the *Starship Enterprise* in the television series *Star Trek*.
Spuds Mackenzie	The bull terrier, who was known as the "Party Animal," and advertised Budweiser beer in television commercials.
Squeaky	The little girl in the 1989 animated movie *All Dogs Go To Heaven*.
Stinkey	The name of a dog in the television series *Dharma & Greg*.
Striker	The call sign of a pilot in the movie *Top Gun*.
Strongheart	The German shepherd who was the first canine hero of feature films.
Sugar Pie	The name of Anna Nicole Smith's dog from the television series *The Anna Nicole Show*.
Sundance Kid	The western outlaw played by Robert Redford in the 1969 movie *Butch Cassidy and the Sundance Kid*. (See BUTCH CASSIDY.)
Susan Hayward	Academy Award winner, Best Actress, for her role in the movie, *I Want to Live* (1958).
Susan Sarandon	Academy Award winner, Best Actress, for her role in the movie *Dead Man Walking* (1995).
Sylvester	A black-and-white cat who has appeared often with Tweety Pie, the canary, in many Warner Brothers' animated cartoons.
Sylvester Stallone	The actor who has starred in the ROCKY movies and the RAMBO movies.
T. C.	THOMAS MAGNUM's friend, who pilots a helicopter in the television series *Magnum, P.I.*

Tar Baby	The inanimate baby who mystified all the animals in the Walt Disney movie *Song of the South* (1946); based on Joel Chandler Harris's stories.
Terminator	Title character in a movie series starring Arnold Schwarzenegger.
Thumper	The rabbit in Walt Disney's animated movie *Bambi* (1942). (See BAMBI.)
Tigger	The bouncy tiger in the animated television versions of A. A. Milne's Winnie-the-Pooh stories.
Tim	The star of the television series *Home Improvement*.
Timon	Pumbaa's sidekick who befriends Simba in the Walt Disney animated movie *The Lion King*.
Tinkerbell	The tiny fairy in the Walt Disney movie *Peter Pan*.
Toby	KUNTA KINTE'S name as a slave in the television mini-series *Roots* (1977).
Tom Hanks	Academy Award winner, Best Actor, for his roles in the movies, *Philadelphia* (1993), and *Forrest Gump* (1994).
Tom	The famous cat who, with his partner, the mouse JERRY, has appeared in numerous MGM, and later Hanna-Barbera animated cartoons.
Tonto	The LONE RANGER'S Indian companion in both the movie and the television series about *The Lone Ranger*.
Tootsie	The man-turned-woman, played by DUSTIN HOFFMAN in the movie *Tootsie*.

Toto — Dorothy's dog in the movie *The Wizard of Oz* (1939).

Tramp — The stray dog who fell in love with LADY, the pretty cocker spaniel, in Walt Disney Productions' animated feature *Lady and the Tramp*.

Trapper — HAWKEYE'S buddy in the television series *M*A*S*H*.

Victor McLaglen — Academy Award winner, Best Actor, for his role in the movie, *The Informer* (1935).

Vivian Leigh — Academy Award winner, Best Actress, for her roles in the movies, *Gone With the Wind* (1939), and *A Streetcar Named Desire* (1951).

Wallace Beery — Academy Award winner, Best Actor, for his role in the movie, *The Champ* (1931).

Wally (Cleaver) — BEAVER'S older brother in the television series *Leave It to Beaver*.

Warner Baxter — Academy Award winner, Best Actor, for his role in the movie, *In Old Arizona* (1928).

Wile E. Coyote — The hapless pursuer of Road Runner in a series of animated films.

William Hurt — Academy Award winner, Best Actor, for his role in the movie, *Kiss of the Spider Woman* (1985).

Wilson — TIM and JILL'S next door neighbor in the television series *Home Improvement*.

Wishbone — A small dog who is the title character of the children's television series *Wishbone*.

Wonder Woman — Title character of the superhero played by Lynda Carter in the 1970s television series based on the comic book heroine of the 1940s.

Xena — Title character of the television series *Xena, Warrior Princess*.

Yoda — LUKE SKYWALKER'S mentor who trains Luke to become a JEDI in the movies *The Empire Strikes Back* and *Return of the Jedi*.

Yogi (Bear) — The hero of the animated television cartoon *Yogi Bear*, who lives in Jellystone National Park.

Yukon King — The husky who aided Sergeant Preston of the Northwest Mounted Police in his television show, *Sergeant Preston of the Yukon*.

Yul Brynner — Academy Award winner, Best Actor, for his role in the movie, *The King and I* (1956).

Zazu — Scar's assistant in the Walt Disney animated movie *The Lion King*.

Zeus — One of the two Doberman pinschers owned by Robin Masters on the television series *Magnum P.I.* (See APOLLO.)

CHAPTER 12

Locations and Places

You don't know what a country we have got till you start prowling around it. Personally, I like the small places and sparsely populated states.

Will Rogers

If you're caught without a map or atlas, check this chapter—you'll find that little spot you've been looking for. Or, pick your favorite place in the world as your pet's name. Be creative, be original, be anything or anywhere you want—just don't let your pet be nameless.

Locations and Places

Acapulco (Mexico)
Africa
Alamo (Texas)
Albany
Amazon (a river in South America)
America
Angola
Asia
Aspen (Colorado)
Austin (Texas)
Azores
Bahamas
Bali
Baltic
Bangkok (Thailand)
Bangladesh
Barbados
Bayou (a marshy creek)
Beijing (China)
Belgium
Belize
Bermuda
Bogota (Colombia)
Bombay
Boston
Brazil

Brazos (a river in Texas)
Broadway (the "Great White Way" in New York City)
Brooklyn (New York)
Burgundy (a region in France)
Burma
Butte (Montana)
Cairo (Eygpt)
Calgary (Canada)
Camelot (the legendary capital of Arthur's kingdom)
Cancun (Mexico)
Carmel (California)
Carolina
Cayman (Islands)
Chad
Chelsea (a district in London and in New York City)
Cheyenne (Wyoming)
Chile
China
Colorado (Rado)
Congo
Cozumel (Mexico)
D. C. (Washington, District of Columbia)
Dakota

Locations and Places

Dallas (Texas)

Delaware (Dele)

Denmark

Denver

Dixie (a traditional name for the South)

Downtown

Egypt

El Dorado (the legendary City of Gold of the Spanish explorers)

Fargo (North Dakota)

Fiji

Florida

France

Freeway (a limited-access highway)

Fresno (California)

Gabon

Geneva

Georgia

Ghana

Granada

Greece

Guinea

Guyana

Hawaii

Hilton (a hotel chain)

Holland (The Netherlands)

Houston

Hyatt (a hotel chain)

India

Ixtapa (Mexico)

Jakarta

Jamaica

Jordan

Juneau (Alaska)

Junk Yard Cat

Junk Yard Dog

K. C. (Kansas City, Kansas and Missouri)

Katamandu (Nepal)

Kaunai

Kenya

Keys (a chain of islands off the southern tip of Florida)

Klondike

Kong (Hong Kong)

L. A. (Los Angeles, California)

Laos

Libya

Loch Ness (Scotland)

Madison

Madrid (Spain)

Mali

Malta

Manzanillo (Mexico)

Marriott (a hotel chain)

Maui

Mazatlan (Mexico)

Memphis (Tennessee)

Monaco

Montana

Morocco

Nassau

Nepal

Nevada

Nieman Marcus (an upscale department store)

Niger

Nile (a river in East Africa)

Oahu

Oman

Osaka

Oslo (Norway)

P. V. (Puerto Vallarta, Mexico)

Palau

Panama

Paris

Pecos (Texas)

Peking (China)

Persia

Peru

Phoenix (Arizona)

Pompeii

Rado (Colorado)

Randolph

Reno

Reykjavik (Iceland)

Rio (Rio de Janeiro, Brazil)

Ritz (a luxury hotel)

Samoa

Sedona (a city in Arizona)

Seoul

Shade

Shiloh (the name for cities in Tennessee and Palestine)

Siam

Sidney (Australia)

Sierra

Spain

Sudan

Tahiti

Taipei

Taj Mahal (an Islamic monument built in India in the seventeenth century)

Tara (a village in Ireland)

Terlingua (a town in Texas)

Locations and Places

Texas (Tex)

Tianjin

Tibet

Timbuktu (a city in Mali)

Togo (an African nation)

Tonga

Touraine (France)

Tripoli (Libya)

Troy (New York)

Tulsa

Turkey

Tuvalu

Uganda

Utah

Vegas (Las Vegas, Nevada)

Venice (Italy)

Virginia

Waco (Texas)

Wales

Yemen

Yukon

Yuma (Arizona)

Zaire

Zambia

"Brooklyn"

"Fraidy"

CHAPTER 13

Unusual Names and Nicknames

. . . people select names for some private reason or for no reason at all—except to arouse a visitor's curiosity, so that he will exclaim, "Why in the world do you call your dog that?" The cryptic name their dogs October, Bennet's Aunt, Three Fifteen, Doc Knows, Tuesday, Home Fried, Opus 38, Ask Leslie, and Thanks for the Home Run, Emil. I make it a point simply to pat these unfortunate dogs on the head, ask no questions of their owners, and go about my business.

James Thurber
from *How to Name a Dog*

One of my clients once told me she had considered renaming her dog after she found herself standing in her front yard, at midnight, calling "Here, Woogie Woogie!"

But if you're not likely to be concerned with what other people think, feel free to get as outrageous as your imagination will allow.

Unusual Names and Nicknames

A. J.	Belle	Bomber	Bucky
AboGato	Beta	Boo	Bud
Ace	Bif	BooBoo	Buddy
Al Fresco	Big Boss	Boogie	Buddyweiser
Al Poochino	Big Boy	Boogie Boy	Buffer
Alfie	Big Daddy	Booh	Buffin
Alley Cat	Big Foot	Booker	Buffy
Allie	Big Guy	Boomer	Bugsy
Alpha	Big John	Boots	Bullet
Animal	Big Red	Bootsie	Bun Bun
Apache	Big'un	Boozer	Buster
April	Bigbird	Bowser	Buster Black
Arlee	Bigun	Boy	Butch
Aztec	Billy Bob	Boy Dog	Butterfingers
B. B.	Bingo	Boz	Butthead
B. J.	Binky	Bozo	Button(s)
Babbs	Blaze	Bravo	Buzz
Bad Debt	Bliss	Briana	Ca Cee
Bandi	Blitz	Bro	Cadi
Bark-ley	Blood	Bubah	Cai
Barks A Lot	Blowout	Bubba	Cali
Bartholo-mew	Blue	Bubbles	Calley
Beau Beau	Bo	Buck	Callie
Beaux	Bobbi	Buckaroo	Cally
Bebe	Bobby	Bucko	Candi
Bee	Bobo	Buckshot	Capoochino

Cappy	Cheebe	Cinder	D. D.
Caprice	Cheers	Cio Cio Sam	Daffy
Captain Happy	Chelsea	Cisco	Dagney
Career Girl	Chelsey	Clawdius	Dahli
Cat #1	Chelsia	Clazy	Dar
Cat #2	Chelsie	Club	Dawg
Cat Astrophe	Cheri	Co Co	Dax
Cati	Cherokee	Coco	Daze
Catpuccino	Chew-chee	Coco Bear	Deli
Catrinka	Chickie	Codie	Destiny
Catsanova	Chicle	Cody	Dexter
Catty Wompus	Chief	Collie	Digi (Digital)
Cee Gee	Chilla	Comanche	Dingbat
Chainsaw	Chimpy	Cooler	Dobie
Chamois	Chris	Corker	Dobie Won Kanobi
Chance	Chrisitiana	Corky	Donation
Chancy	Chrissy	Cotton	Doo Dah
Chap	Christabel	Cottontail	Doodle
Chapin	Christmas	Cowboy	Doodles
Chappy	Chu Chen	Crash	Doogie Bowser
Chaps	Chu Chu	Cricket	Doozie
Charlette	Chuckles	Critter	Dough Boy
Charley	Chula	Crockett Cat	Doxy
Charli	Chump	Crystal	Dude
Charlie	Chuska	Cuki	Dudette
Charmin	Cici	D. C.	Dudlee

Unusual Names and Nicknames

Duffie	Freebee	Hef	Joe Cool
Duffy	Friday	Hekter	Joker
Dumpster	Fusby	Helen Dalmation	Jossie
Duster	G'Day	Hi Pockets	Jr.
Dusty	Ged	Hissy Fit	Judi
Dutch	Ghillie	Hojo	Jukie
Dweebe	Gi Gi	Holly Hobbles	Jumbo
Dy	Gink	Hooter	Just A Minute
Elkie	Girl	Howie	Justa Cat
Esti	Girl Dog	Iggy	Justa Dog
Eulika	Gizmo	Ima Cat	Justice
Ewoke	Goober	Inca	K. C.
Exxene	Goofie Bear	Itty Bitty	K. D.
Farkle	Gorbe Chow	J. D.	K. J.
Fella	Grammar	J. J.	Kadee
Ferret Fawcett	Gringo	Jammer	Kali
Fifi	Grommet	Jane Doe	Kally
Fila	Groove Dog	Jasmine	Kat
Flakes	Groovey	Jenn-i-purr	Kater
Flaps	Grrrr	Jetta	Keba
Flower	H. T.	Jillsy	Keesha
Fluffer	Hailey	Jimbo	Keeta
Fluffles	Half Pint	Jingles	Kelli
Flush	Hamlet	Jinx	Ker Plop
Fragment	Hawg	Jip	Kevin Bacon
Fraidy	Hazard	Jo Jo	Key Key

Keys	Lady Lin	Maudie	Miss Fortune
Kiki	Lappy	Maverick	Miss Kitty
Kinki	Legacy	Maxi	Miss Take
Kit Kat	Lexie	Mc Gruffen	Miss Tickle
Kitsy	Li'l Guy	Me Too	Missy
Kitt	Li'l Honeysuckle	Meathead	Misty
Kittens	Lia	Meetsie	Mitch
Kitter	Liberace	Meow	Mitzi
Kitti	Little B	Meow Say Tongue	Mitzie
Kitty Boy	Little Bit	Mercy	Mitzu
Kitty Carlyle	Little Girl	Merry Christmas	Mixture
Kitty Q	Little Kitty	Mew	Mo
Kitty Tom	Lobo	Mew Mew	Mo Jo
Knuckles	Lolo	Mia Ferret	Moe
Kobi	Lou Lou	Middie	Moffie
Kodak	Lutino	Miffy	Mofford
Kokomo	Mac Duff	Milo	Molley
Kringles	Mackie	Mimi	Moma
Kristil	Maddie	Mimie	Momma Dog (Cat)
Kuchen	MagnifiCat	Minnesota Cats	Moo Moo
Kwik	Mail	Minni	Mopsy
Kyrie	Majic	Minnie	Mortikie
Lace	Mama Trouble	Minnie Paws	Morty
Lacey	Mao Tse Tongue	Miss Behavin'	Moss
Ladi	Mary Dog	Miss Chevious	Mouse Tse Tung
Lady Gal	Mate	Miss Demeanor	Mr. Cuddles

Mr. Kitty	Okie	Polecat	Punkie
Mr. Stubbs	Ombre	Poli	Punky
Mr. T	Owlpuccino	Polson	Pup
Mrs. T	P. B.	Ponch	Pupdog
Ms. Muffet	P. C.	Poo Bee Bear	Pupper
Mudd	P. C. Jr.	Pooch	Puppy
Muff	P. J.	Poochie	Pups
Muffer	Pandy	Poochkie	Pupster
Muffett	Papito	Pooh	Pupus
Muffie	Papoose	Pooh Bear	Purr
Muffy	Paraphernalia (Pari)	Pooky	Purr Son
Muggs	Paw Pet	Pooper	Purrbert
Mugsie	Peace	Poops	Purrsilla
Munchkin	Pebbles	Pooter	Purrsnickitty
Musgly	Pee Dee	Poppy	Puss
Mutzie	Pennie	Potsi	Puss Cat
Navajo	Penny	Pozzo	R. B.
New Kitty	Peppy	Princess Daisy	Rags
Nic Nac	Perky	Princess Josette	Rainbow
Nicky	Petunia	Princess Tiffany	Ralfy
Niki	Phideaux	Priss	Rascal
Nikke	PiCatSo	Prissy	Rasta
No White	Pinky	Pudder	Rat
Nooner	Pitney	Puddy Willow	Ratcat
Odd Ball	Podnah	Puffy	Ratus
Oh No	Pojoo	Pugsly	Raven

Razz	Rockey	Rosie	Sashi
Razzy	Rodeo	Roxie	Sassy
Recount	Rolf	Roxy	Sassy San
Red Neck	Rollie	Rug Rat	Saturday
Reggie	Romer	Ruffles	Saucer
Remington	Roo	S. L. O'Pokey	Sawdust
Ricki	Rootin' Tootin	Saige	Scamp
Ringo	Rosco	Saint Bernie Nard	Scat Cat
Rinky Dink	Roscoe	Samba (o)	Schwatz
Rip	Rose	Sami	Scottie
Rip Van Beagle	Rosebud	Sarg	Sebo

"Splash"

Unusual Names and Nicknames

Seminole	Skippy	Special	Stinker
Serendipity	Skitter	Speckles	Stoney
Shadie	Skitty	Speed Bump	Stormy
Shady	Skunky	Spike	Striker
Shammy	Skwiggles	Spiker	Strubie
Sheba	Slick	Spikey	Stud
Sheeba	Slugger	Spirit	Stymie
Shimmy	Smitty	Splash	Sudi
Shinola	Snapper de Aire	Split	Su-Lin
Shoebutton	Snert	Spooner	Sue E.
Shooter	Snoobie	Sport	Suki
Shorty Bob	Snooker	Sporty	Sundance
Shotie	Snooky	Spring	Sunday
Shu Shu	Snoops	Sprinkle	Sunnie
Si	Snow Bear	Spunky	Sunny
Siah	Snowball	Squeaker	Sunny Cat
Silver Bell	Snubbs	Squeakers	Sunspot
Sioux	Snuff	Squealer	Supplies
Sir Chadwick	Sonny	Squish	Suzie Queen
Sir Woody	Soo	Star	T. C.
Sissie	Soo Shi	Stardust	T. J.
Sissy	Sooka	Starr	Taboo
Sister	Sophistocat	Stash	Taffi
Skeeter	SoSueMe	Static	TAG Heuer
Skinner	Spade	Sterling	Tai
Skipper	Sparky	Stickers	Tally

Tashi	Tipster	Turkey	Wifferdill
Tasi	Tipsy	Tusche	Wild Child
Taski	Tobe	Twerp	Wild Thing
Tatters	Tobi	Twinkle Toes	Wildfire
Tattoo	Tobia	Twit	Willow
Tawnya	Toddy	Tynee	Wimpy
Taz	Tomahawk	Uga	Winkie
Ted E. Bear	Toodles	Velcro	Wisky Blue
Tennie	Toot	Wagley	Wizard
Tex	Toot Toot	Wakedy Yak	Woodsie
Thomas Our Cat	Tootie	Waterford	Woogy
Thunder	Tootsie	Weebles	Woopsie
Tic Tac	Topper	Wetta	Wova
Tick Tock	Torti	Whacker	Wrecks
Ticker	Tortilla	Whampuss	YoYo
Tidbit	Trapper	Whiplash	Zac
Tiffy	Trendsetter	Whisper	Zee
Tikki	Trixie	Whiz Bang	Zero
Tiko	Trooper	Whiz O	Zip
Timex	Trouffels	Why Not	
Tinker	Tuffy	Wicked Wizard	
Tippy	Turbo	Wicket	

CHAPTER 14

Cartoon Characters

Peanuts characters © copyright 1950, 1952, 1958 by United Features Syndicate.

Charles Schultz
from *You Don't Look 35, Charlie Brown*

Your pet may be the perfect Daffy Duck or Road Runner—guaranteed to always make you laugh. But plan ahead! When he or she is testing your patience, a stern "Jughead, I told you to behave" may change your stern countenance into a smiling face.

Cartoon Characters

Al Capp	Cartoonist; creator of "Li'l Abner."
Albert	A main character in "Pogo."
Alley Oop	Title character.
Alvin	A character in *The Chipmunks*.
Andy Capp	Title character.
Angelica Pickles	Character in *Rugrats*.
Animal Crackers	Title character.
Annie (Little Orphan)	Title character.
Archie	Title character.
B. C.	Title character.
Bam Bam	A character in *The Flintstones*.
Barney Google	Title character.
Barney Rubble	A character in *The Flintstones*.
Bart Simpson	Character in *The Simpsons*.
Batman	Title character.
Beetle Bailey	Title character.

Beauregard Bugleboy	A character in "POGO."
Bender	Animated robot on the television series *Futurama*.
Betty	A character in *The Flintstones*.
Betty Boop	Title character.
Beavis	Title character in *Beavis and Butthead*.
Blondie	Title character.
Blossom	Leader of *The Powerpuff Girls*, an animated series.
Bluto	Character in *Popeye*.
Bobby Hill	Peggy and Hank's son on *King of the Hill*.
Bonzo	Title character.
Boris	Character in *Rocky and Bullwinkle*.
Brainey	A character in *The Smurfs*.
Brutus	A villain in *Popeye*.
Bubbles	One of *The Powerpuff Girls*.
Bugs Bunny	Title character.
Bullwinkle Moose	Title character in *Rocky and Bullwinkle*.

Cartoon Characters

Bumstead	DAGWOOD and BLONDIE'S family name.
Buster Brown	Title character.
Buttercup	Another of *The Powerpuff Girls*.
Butthead	Title character in *Beavis and Butthead*.
Buzz Sawyer	Title character.
Calvin	Title character in "Calvin and Hobbes."
Cap Stubbs	Title character.
Captain Marvel	Title character.
Casper	Title character: *Casper the Friendly Ghost*.
Cathy	Title character.
Charlie Brown	Co-star of comic strip and television series *Peanuts*.
Chef (McElroy)	The school chef voiced by Isaac Hayes on *South Park*.
Chip	Title character in *Chip and Dale*.
Chipmunk(s)	Title character(s).
Chucky Finster	Character in *Rugrats*.
Daffy Duck	Title character.

Dagwood	BLONDIE'S husband.
Daisy	DONALD DUCK'S girlfriend.
Daisy Mae	LI'L ABNER'S girlfriend.
Dale	Title character in *Chip and Dale*.
Dennis the Menace	Title character.
Deputy Dawg	Title character.
Dewey	Character in "Donald Duck."
Dick Tracy	Title character.
Dilbert	Title character.
Dinny	ALLEY OOP'S pet dinosaur.
Donald Duck	Title character; also MICKEY MOUSE'S friend.
Doonesbury	Title of strip.
Doug	Title character.
Droopy	Title character.
Elmer Fudd	A character in *Looney Tunes*.
Elwood	Title character.

Cartoon Characters

Farley	Dog in the comic strip "For Better or Worse."
Fearless Fosdick	Character in "Li'l Abner."
Felix the Cat	Title character.
Flash Gordon	Title character.
Flintstone(s)	Title character(s).
Fred Basset	Title character.
Fred	Title character in *The Flintstones*.
Fritz	A character in "The Katzenjammer Kids."
Fritz the Cat	Title character.
Garfield	Title character.
Gertie	Title character in "Gertie, the Trained Dinosaur."
Goofy	A character in "Mickey Mouse."
Gordo	Title character.
Grammy	Title character.
Gumby	Title character in *Gumby and Pokey*.
Gummi Bear	Title character.

Hagar the Horrible	Title character.
Hank Hill	Texan father voiced by Mike Judge on *King of the Hill*.
Hans	A character in "The Katzenjammer Kids."
Happy Hooligan	Title character.
Hazel	Title character.
Heathcliff	Title character.
Heckle and Jeckle	Title characters.
Heifer	Character in *Rocko's Modern Life*.
Henry	Title character.
Hi	Title character of "Hi and Lois."
Hobbes	Title character in "Calvin and Hobbes."
Homer Simpson	Character in *The Simpsons*.
Huckleberry Hound	Title character.
Huey	Character in "Donald Duck."
Ickus	Character in *Real Monsters*.
Ignatz Mouse	Title character.

Jeff	Title character in "Mutt and Jeff."
Jerry	Title character in *Tom and Jerry*.
Jiggs	A character in the cartoon strip "Bringing Up Father."
Joe Cool	SNOOPY's alter ego in *Peanuts*.
Joe Palooka	Title character.
Jughead	A character in "Archie."
Jungle Jim	Title character.
Katzenjammer Kids	Title character(s).
Kenny McCormick	The small boy who dies at the end of every episode of *South Park*.
Krazy Kat	Title character.
Krumb	Character in *Real Monsters*.
Li'l Abner	Title character.
Lil	Character in *Rugrats*.
Linus	A character in comic strip and television series *Peanuts*.
Lisa Simpson	Character in *The Simpsons*.

Little Lulu	Title character.
Lois	Title character in "Hi and Lois."
Louie	Character in "Donald Duck."
Luann	Title character.
Lucy	A character in *Peanuts*.
Maggie	A character in "Bringing Up Father."
Margaret	A character in "Dennis the Menace."
Marge Simpson	Character in *The Simpsons*.
Marmaduke	Title character.
Maw	A character in "Snuffy Smith."
Mickey Mouse	Title character.
Mighty Mouse	Title character.
Minnie Mouse	MICKEY MOUSE'S girlfriend.
Mojo Jojo	The archenemy of *The Powerpuff Girls*.
Moon Mullins	Title character.
Mr. Boffo	Title character.

Cartoon Characters

Mr. Dink	Character in *Doug*.
Mr. Magoo	Title character.
Muddy the Mudskipper	Character in *Ren and Stimpy*.
Mutt	Title character in "Mutt and Jeff."
Nancy	Title character.
Napoleon	Title character.
Natasha	Character in *Rocky and Bullwinkle*.
Nermal	Cat in "Garfield" comics.
Nervy Nat	Title character.
Nudnik	Title character.
Oblina	Character in *Real Monsters*.
Odie	GARFIELD's canine friend.
Offisa Bull Pupp	A character in *Krazy Kat*.
Okefenokee	The setting (a swamp) in the series "Pogo."
Olive Oil	POPEYE's girlfriend.
Opus	The penguin in the comic strip series "Bloom County."

Pasquale	Baby boy in the comic strip "Rose is Rose."
Patrick Star	*SpongeBob's* starfish pal.
Peanuts	Title of comic strip and television series.
Pebbles	A character in the comic strip and television series *The Flintstones*.
Peggy Hill	Texan mother on *King of the Hill*.
Pepe Le Pew	A character in *Looney Tunes*.
Pepe Le Pu	Title character.
Peppermint Patty	A character in the comic strip and television series *Peanuts*.
Petunia Pig	A character in "Porky Pig."
Phil	Character in *Rugrats*.
Philbert	Character in *Rocko's Modern Life*.
Phineas T. Bridgeport	A character in "Pogo."
Pig-Pen	A character in the comic strip and television series *Peanuts*.
Pink Panther	Title character.
Pluto	MICKEY MOUSE'S dog.
Pogo	Title character.

Cartoon Characters

Pokey	Title character in *Gumby and Pokey*.
Popeye	Title character.
Porkchop	Character in *Doug*.
Porky Pig	Title character.
Prince Valiant	Title character.
Professor Utonium	Creator/father figure to *The Powerpuff Girls*.
Quincy	The iguana in the comic strip "Fox Trot."
Ready	Title character in "Ruff and Ready."
Ren	The skinny chihuahua on *Ren and Stimpy*.
Road Runner	Title character.
Rocko	Title character in *Rocko's Modern Life*.
Rocky (the Flying Squirrel)	Title character in *Rocky and Bullwinkle*.
Rose	Title character in "Rose is Rose."
Ruff	(1) A character in "Dennis the Menace"; (2) title character in "Ruff and Ready."
Sally	A character in the comic strip and television series *Peanuts*.

Schroeder	A character in the comic strip and television series *Peanuts*.
Scooby Doo	Title character.
Simon	Title character, *The Chipmunks*.
Simple J. Malarkey	A character in "Pogo."
Sluggo	(1) Sarge's dog in the comic strip "Beetle Bailey." (2) NANCY'S friend in "Nancy."
Smithers	Character in *The Simpsons*.
Smurf	Title character.
Smurfette	A character in *The Smurfs*.
Snoopy	Title character in the comic strip and television series *Peanuts*.
Snuffy Smith	Title character.
Solomon	Title character.
Space Ghost	Title character.
Speedy Gonzales	Title character.
Spike	A character in *Tom and Jerry*; a character in *Rugrats*.

Cartoon Characters

SpongeBob SquarePants	A pants-wearing sponge who is the title character of the animated series.
Squidward Tentacles	An unfriendly neighborhood squid on *SpongeBob SquarePants*.
Steve Canyon	Title character.
Stimpy	The cat voiced by Billy West in *Ren and Stimpy*.
Stinky	Character in *Doug*.
Susie	Character in *Rugrats*.
Sweet Pea	Character in "Popeye."
Sylvester	Title character.
Sylvia	Title character.
Tarzan	Title character.
Tintin	Title character.
Tippie	Title character in a comic strip no longer in print.
Tom	Title character in *Tom and Jerry*.
Tommy Pickles	Character in *Rugrats*.
Trudy	Title character.

Tweetie Pie	A character in the comic strip and animated cartoon *Sylvester the Cat*.
Veronica	A character in "Archie."
Wile E. Coyote	A character in the comic strip and animated cartoon *The Road Runner*.
Wiley Catt	A character in "Pogo."
Wilma	A character in the comic strip and television series *The Flintstones*.
Wimpie	A character in the comic strip and animated cartoon *Popeye*.
Winnie-the-Pooh	Title character.
Wizard of Id	Title character.
Woodstock	A character in the comic strip and television series *Peanuts*.
Woody the Woodpecker	Title character.
Yogi	Title character in *Yogi the Bear*.
Zero	A character in "Beetle Bailey."
Ziggy	Title character.

"Primadonna"

CHAPTER 15

Just for Fun

But I tell you, a cat needs a name that's particular,
A name that's peculiar, and more dignified,
Else how can he keep up his tail perpendicular,
Or spread out his whiskers, or cherish his pride?

T. S. Eliot
from *Old Possum's Book of Practical Cats*

A school mascot or the name of a singer may become your new pet's name. Use this short chapter to give you some ideas; there are only a few names suggested here to get you started on your own list.

ASSORTED NAMES

Ace	Cribbage	Jive	Rock-ola
Baccarat	Cue Ball	Joker	Sailor
Backgammon	D. J.	Keno	Scrabble
Ballerina	Danny Boy	Lawyer	Sergeant Pepper
Banjo	Dealer	Lotto	Shooter
Banker	Diamond	Manager	Slot
Bartender	Dice	Payout	Spade
Bill Bailey	Disco	Pilot	Spin
Blackjack	Doc	Player	Tango
Bluegrass	Floorman	Poker	Tom Dooley
Boogie	Gig 'Em	Primadonna	Trifecta
Card	Gin Rummy	Prof	Trucker
Cha Cha	Jackpot	Purse	Walin' Jennings
Chip	Jazz	Reel	Way Out Willie
Club	Jitter Bug	Rock	Winner

ENTERTAINERS—PAST AND PRESENT

Alan Jackson
Barbara Mandrell
Barbra Streisand
B. B. King
Beatle(s)
Bee Gee(s)
Bette Midler
Bill Cosby
Bill Murray
Billy Joel
Billy Ray Cyrus
Bing Crosby
Blood, Sweat and
   Tears
Bob Dylan
Bobbie Gentry
Bobby Goldsboro
Bob Hope
Bon Jovi
Bonnie Raitt
Brenda Lee
Bruce Springsteen
Buck Owens
Buddy Hackett

Buddy Holly
Carole King
Charlie Daniels
Charlie Pride
Charlie Rich
Cher
Chet Atkins
Chris Isaak
Chubby Checker
Chuck Berry
Clint Black
Conway Twitty
Crystal Gayle
Dale Evans
Dan Ayckroyd
David Cooperfield
David Bowie
David Letterman
Dean Martin
Diana Ross
Dolly Parton
Dottie West
Dusty Springfield
Dwight Yoakam

Eagle(s)
Eddie Murphy
Elton John
Elvis Presley
Emmylou Harris
Eric Clapton
Ernest Tubb
Fleetwood Mac
Floyd (Pink Floyd)
Frank Sinatra
Frankie Avalon
Fred Astaire
Gallagher
Garth Brooks
Gene Autry
Gene Kelly
George Burns
George Carlin
George Harrison
George Strait
Gilda Radner
Ginger Rogers
Glen Campbell
Gracie Allen

Groucho Marx
Hank Snow
Hank Williams
Harpo Marx
Harry Chapin
Jack Benny
James Taylor
Jay Leno
Jerry Lewis
Jerry Lee Lewis
Jerry Seinfeld
Jimmy Buffett
Joan Baez
Joan Rivers
Jimmy Dean
John Denver
Judy Collins
Judy Garland
Julio Iglesias
June Carter
Kenny Rogers
Kris Kristofferson
Lawrence Welk
Lee Greenwood

Lily Tomlin	Milton Berle	Reba McEntire	Stevie Wonder
Linda Ronstadt	Naomi Judd	Red Buttons	Tanya Tucker
Liberace	Natalie Cole	Red Skelton	Tennessee Ernie Ford
Lionel Richie	Nat "King" Cole	Ricky Van Shelton	Tex Ritter
Liza Minnelli	Neil Sedaka	Ringo Starr	Tina Turner
Loretta Lynn	Olivia Newton-John	Rod Stewart	Tom T. Hall
Louis Armstrong	Otis Redding	Robert Earl Keen	Tony Bennett
Lyle Lovett	Patsy Cline	Ronnie Milsap	Travis Tritt
Lynn Anderson	Patty Loveless	Roseanne Cash	Trisha Yearwood
Mac Davis	Paul Anka	Roy Acuff	U2
Madonna	Paul Simon	Roy Clark	Van Halen
Marie Osmond	Paul McCartney	Roy Orbison	Vince Gill
Marty Robbins	Pavarotti	Roy Rogers	Wayne Newton
Mel Tillis	Peter, Paul & Mary	Sam Cooke	Whitney Houston
Merle Haggard	Phil Collins	Sammy Davis Jr.	Willie Nelson
Merle Travis	Randy Travis	Selena	Wynonna Judd
Michael Bolton	Ray Charles	Sonny Bono	
Michael Jackson	Ray Price	Steely Dan	
Mick Jagger	Ray Stevens	Stevie Ray Vaughn	

COMPOSERS

Andrew Lloyd Webber	British composer (b. 1948).
Bach	German composer (1685–1750).
Beethoven	German composer (1770–1827).
Cole Porter	American composer (1893–1964).
George Gershwin	American composer (1898–1937).
Irving Berlin	American composer (1888–1989).
Mozart	Austrian composer (1756–1791).
Noel Coward	British composer (1899–1973).

SCHOOL AND COLLEGE MASCOTS AND NICKNAMES

Aggie	Devil	Pacer	Sooner
Bevo	Gator	Panther	Spartan
Big Al	Grizzly	Racer	Titan
Bomber	Hoosier	Rambler	Trojan
Blazer	Horned Toad	Razorback	Viking
Bruin	Husky	Red Raider	Wahoo
Cadet	Ichabod	Rocket	
Charger	Nittany Lion	Reville	
Demon	Jasper	Seminole	

"Peter, Paul & Mary"

"Slam Dunk"

CHAPTER 16

Sports

The game ain't over till it's over.

Yogi (Lawrence Peter) Berra

Throughout the past century, sports has played a big part in our lives. Whether you are an avid sports buff or a part-time fan keeping up with your favorite team, consider some of these entries in your selection of your pet's name.

A. J. Foyt	A famous race car driver; four-time Indy 500 winner.
Ace	In tennis, an unreturnable serve.
Adidas	A brand of athletic wear.
Al Unser	Auto Racing: One of IndyCar's top twenty drivers.
Al Worthington	Baseball: A pitcher for the Giants in the 50s and the Twins and the White Sox in the 60s.
Alessandro Zanardi	Auto Racing: Won the Indy Car in 1997 and 1998.
Allison Nicholas	Golf: Winner of the U.S. Women's Open in 1997.
Amy Alcott	Golf: 1980 U.S. Women's Open Champion.
Andre Agassi	Tennis: Won Wimbledon in 1992, and was the U.S. Open Champion in 1994 and 1999.
Andre Ware	Football: 1989 winner of the Heisman Memorial Trophy.
Annika Sorenstam	Golf: Winner of the 1995 and 1996 Women's Open.
Archie Griffin	Football: 1974 and 1975 winner of the Heisman Memorial Trophy (Ohio State University).
Arnold Palmer	Golf: Winner of four Masters Tournaments, one U.S. Open, and two British Open Tournaments.
Babe Ruth	Baseball: One of the most famous all-time athletes, Ruth hit sixty home runs in 1927 while playing for the New York Yankees.

Balk	In baseball, an incomplete or misleading motion.
Barry Bonds	Baseball: Single season home run record holder.
Barry Sanders	Football: 1988 winner of the Heisman Memorial Trophy (Oklahoma State University).
Bart Starr	Football: Hall of Famer; active 1965 to 1973; associated mainly with the Green Bay Packers.
Batter	In baseball, the player attempting to hit the ball.
Bear Bryant	Football: Coach at Texas A&M University in the 50s and at the University of Alabama in the 60s, 70s, and 80s.
Ben Crenshaw	Golf: Won the Masters Tournament in 1995.
Ben Hogan	Golf: Winner of four U.S. Opens. In 1953, he won the Masters, the U.S. Open, and the British Open.
Bernhard Langer	Golf: Won the Masters Tournament in 1993.
Betsy King	Golf: Winner of the 1989 and 1990 U.S. Women's Open.
Billy Jean King	Tennis: Winner of several indoor, U.S. Open, and Wimbledon titles (among others) during the 1960s and 1970s.
Billy Sims	Football: 1978 winner of the Heisman Memorial Trophy.
Birdie	In golf, a score of one under PAR.
Bo Jackson	Football: 1985 Heisman Memorial Trophy winner (Auburn University).

Sports

Bob Cousy	Basketball: A Boston Celtics standout, Cousy scored fifty points in a 1953 playoff game—a record at the time.
Bobby Hull	Ice Hockey: Player, elected to the Hall of Fame, having spent the most productive years with the Chicago Blackhawks.
Bobby Labonte	Auto Racing: Won the Winston Cup Championship in 2000.
Bobby Mitchell	Football: First black player to be a member of the Washington Redskins; he was later elected to the Hall of Fame.
Bobby Unser	Auto Racing: One of IndyCar's top twenty drivers.
Bogey	In golf, a score of one over PAR.
Boog Powell	Baseball: Outfielder for the Baltimore Orioles in the 60s and 70s; best known for his appearance on Miller Lite beer commercials.
Boris Becker	Tennis: Three-time winner of Wimbledon (1985, 1986, and 1989) and winner of the U.S. Open (1989).
Boxer	In boxing, one who fights with his fists.
Brett Hull	Hockey: Won the Hart Trophy-MVP in 1991 (St. Louis).
Bunker	In golf, a sand TRAP.
Cal Ripkin	Baseball: On September 6, 1995, broke Lou Gehrig's record of 2,130 for most consecutive games played.
Carl Lewis	Track and Field: World record holder in the 100-Meter Dash and the 200-Meter Dash (1984 Summer Olympic Games).

Carlos Delgado — Baseball: Winner of the Hank Aaron Award in 2000.

Carson Palmer — Football: Winner of the 2002 Heisman Memorial Trophy (USC).

Casey Stengel — Baseball: Former manager of the New York Yankees; led his team to ten American League pennant titles from 1949 to 1980.

Cassius Clay — See MUHAMMAD ALI.

Catcher — In baseball, the player who receives the pitches from the PITCHER.

Center — In football, the player who hands the ball to the QUARTERBACK.

Charles Barkley — Basketball: NBA MVP for 1993 (Phoenix Suns).

Charles White — Football: 1979 winner of the Heisman Memorial Trophy (USC).

Charles Woodson — Football: Winner of the 1997 Heisman Memorial Trophy (Michigan).

Charley Taylor — Football: A receiver for the Washington Redskins who caught a record 649 passes from 1964 to 1977.

Charlie Ward — Football: 1993 winner of the Heisman Memorial Trophy (Florida State University).

Chris Evert — Tennis: Winner of several indoor, U.S. Open, and Wimbledon titles (among others) during the 1970s and 1980s.

Chris Pronger — Hockey: Won the Hart Trophy-MVP in 2000 (St. Louis).

Chris Weinke — Football: Winner of the 2000 Heisman Memorial Trophy (Florida State).

Sports

Corey Pavin	Golf: Won the U.S. Open in 1995.
Dale Earnhardt	Auto Racing: Won the Winston Cup Championship 7 times, winning his last Championship in 1994.
Dale Jarrett	Auto Racing: Winston Cup Champion in 1999 and won the Daytona 500 in 2000 at the Daytona International Speedway.
Damon Hill	Auto Racing: Won the World Grand Prix in 1996.
Dan Marino	Football: Leader in passing in the NFL.
Danny Wuerffel	Football: Winner of the 1996 Heisman Memorial Trophy (Florida).
David Robinson	Basketball: NBA Rookie of the Year in 1989–1990; 1991 rebound leader; NBA MVP in 1995 (San Antonio Spurs).
Davis Love III	Golf: Won the U.S. P.G.A. Championship in 1997.
Desmond Howard	Football: 1991 winner of the Heisman Memorial Trophy (Michigan); NFL Superbowl MVP in 1996.
Dick Butkus	Football: Hall of Famer; active 1965 to 1973; associated mainly with Chicago Bears.
Dizzy Dean	Baseball: Winner of National League's Most Valuable Player Award, 1934.
Dominik Hasek	Hockey: Won the Hart Trophy-MVP in 1997, and again in 1998 (Buffalo).
Doug Flutie	Football: 1984 Heisman Memorial Trophy winner (Boston College).

Dribble	In basketball, bouncing the ball on the floor.
Driver	In golf, the club normally used on the tee box for attaining distance.
Eagle	In golf, a score of two under PAR.
Earl Campbell	Football: 1977 Heisman Memorial Trophy winner (University of Texas).
Eddie George	Football: 1995 winner of the Heisman Memorial Trophy (Ohio State).
Emmit Smith	All-time NFL rushing leader and NFL Superbowl MVP in 1993.
Eric Crouch	Football: Winner of the 2001 Heisman Memorial Trophy (Nebraska).
Eric Lindros	Hockey: Won the Hart Trophy-MVP in 1995 (Philadelphia).
Ernie Banks	Baseball: Hit 512 National League home runs.
Ernie Els	Golf: Won the U.S. Open in 1994 and again in 1997. Also won British Open in 2002.
Ervin Johnson	Basketball: NBA MVP for 1990 (Los Angeles Lakers).
Evonne Goolagong	Tennis: Winner at Wimbledon in 1971 and 1980.
Extra Point	In football, scoring a point after a TOUCHDOWN.
Fastball	In baseball, a PITCH thrown at a high rate of speed.
Featherweight	In boxing, a BOXER weighing between 118 and 127 pounds.
Florence Griffith Joyner	Track and Field: 1988 Olympic gold medalist.

Floyd Patterson	Boxing: World HEAVYWEIGHT champion, 1956 to 1959, 1960 to 1962.
Fly Ball	In baseball, a pitch that is hit high into the air.
Flyweight	In boxing, a BOXER in the lightest weight class (weighing 112 pounds or less).
Fran Tarkenton	Football: A leading NFL touchdown passer and leader in passing yards.
Fred Couples	Golf: Won the Masters Tournament in 1992.
Frisbee	A brand of toy that resembles a "flying saucer."
Fullback	In football, a player in the BACKFIELD.
Fumble	In football, the act of an offensive ball carrier dropping the ball.
Fuzzy Zoeller	Golf: Winner of the 1979 Masters and the 1984 U.S. Open.
Gary Player	Golf: 1962 and 1972 P.G.A. Champion, winner of the 1965 U.S. Open, the 1961, 1974, and 1978 Masters, and the 1959, 1968, and 1974 British Open.
George Blanda	Football: Long-time NFL leader in points scored.
George Foreman	Boxing: World HEAVYWEIGHT champion, 1970 to 1973.
George Rogers	Football: 1980 winner of the Heisman Memorial Trophy (South Carolina).
Gil de Ferran	Auto Racing: Won the Indy Car in 2000.

Gino Torretta	Football: 1992 winner of the Heisman Memorial Trophy (Miami).
Goal	In ice hockey, the net into which players try to advance a PUCK. In basketball, the HOOP into which players throw a ball.
Goalie	In ice hockey, the player who defends the GOAL.
Gordie Howe	Hockey: Won the Hart Trophy-MVP in 1952, 1953, 1957, 1958, 1960, and again in 1963 (Detroit).
Greg Norman	Golf: Won the British Open in 1986 and 1993.
Grounder	In baseball, a ball hit on the ground by the BATTER.
Gutter	In bowling, the area on either side of the lane.
Hakeem Olajuwon	Basketball: NBA MVP for 1994 (Houston Rockets).
Hale Irwin	Golf: Won the U.S. Open in 1990.
Halfback	In football, a player in the BACKFIELD.
Hand-off	In football, one offensive player giving the ball to another offensive player.
Hank Aaron	Baseball: Hall of Famer and holder of the following records: Home runs (1st), Runs scored (2nd), and Hits (3rd). In 1999 major league baseball instituted the Hank Aaron Award for the best hitters of the National and American Leagues.
Hazard	An obstacle on a golf course.

Sports

Heavyweight	In boxing, the class of BOXERS in the heaviest weight class, weighing over 175 pounds.
Herschel Walker	Football: 1982 Heisman Memorial Trophy winner (University of Georgia).
Hit-and-Run	In baseball, a play in which the runner progresses to the next base simultaneously with the BATTER hitting the PITCH.
Hobie Cat	A brand of sailboat.
Hollis Stacy	Golf: 1977 and 1978 U.S. Women's Open champion.
Home Run	In baseball, a play in which the ball hit by the BATTER allows him to proceed around all three bases safely to home plate.
Homer	See HOME RUN.
Hoop	In basketball, the goal.
Ian Baker-Finch	Golf: Won the British Open in 1991.
Ian Woosnam	Golf: Won the Masters Tournament in 1991.
Interception	In football, a play in which a defensive player catches a pass in the air.
Jack Dempsey	Boxing: World HEAVYWEIGHT champion, 1919 to 1926.
Jack Nicklaus	Golf: Winner of the following tournaments: six Masters, four U.S. Opens, five PGA's, and three British Opens.
Jackie Joyner-Kersee	Track and Field: 1988 Olympic goal medalist.

Jacques Villeneuve	Auto Racing: Won the World Grand Prix in 1997.
Jan Stephenson	Golf: 1983 U.S. Women's Open champion.
Jana Novotna	Tennis: Won the Women's Wimbledon Championship in 1998.
Jane Geddes	Golf: 1986 U.S. Women's Open champion.
Janet Alex	Golf: 1982 U.S. Women's Open champion.
Jaromir Jagr	Hockey: Won the Hart Trophy-MVP in 1999 (Pittsburgh).
Jeff Gordon	Auto Racing: Won the Winston Cup Championship in 1995, 1997, and 1998.
Jerry Rice	Football: NFL Superbowl MVP in 1988.
Jesse Owens	Track and Field: Winner of four Olympic gold medals in 1936.
Jim Brown	Football: Professional football Hall of Famer; Cleveland Browns, 1957 to 1965.
Jim Thorpe	Pentathlon and Decathlon: 1912 Olympics in Stockholm, Sweden.
Jimmy Vasser	Auto Racing: Won the Indy Car in 1996.
Joe DiMaggio	Baseball: Former New York Yankees outfielder; hit safely in 56 consecutive baseball games.
Joe Frazier	Boxing: World HEAVYWEIGHT champion, 1970 to 1973.
Joe Louis	Boxing: World HEAVYWEIGHT champion from 1937 to 1950.

Sports

Joe Montana	Football: Three-time MVP of Super Bowl Championship teams.
Joe Namath	Football: The New York Jets QUARTERBACK and Hall of Famer (1985); led his team to a 16-7 victory over the Baltimore Colts in the 1969 Super Bowl.
John Daly	Golf: Won the U.S. P.G.A. in 1991, won the British Open in 1995.
John Elway	Football: NFL Super Bowl MVP in 1998.
Johnny Bench	Baseball: Former catcher for the Cincinnati Reds; MVP twice.
Johnny Rutherford	Auto Racing: One of IndyCar's top twenty drivers.
Jose Maria Olazabal	Golf: Won the Masters Tournament in 1994 and again in 1999.
Juan Montoya	Auto Racing: Won the Indy in 1999.
Julie Inkster	Golf: Winner of the 1999 U.S. Women's Open.
Julius Irving	Basketball: Third lifetime NBA leading scorer (30,026 points through 1988 season).
Jump Shot	In basketball, a play in which the ball is propelled toward the GOAL while the player is airborne.
Justin Leonard	Golf: Won the British Open in 1997.
Kareem Abdul-Jabbar	Basketball: Lew Alcindor; Individual NBA scoring champion 1960 to 1972; Milwaukee Bucks.

Karl Malone	Basketball: NBA MVP for 1997 (Utah Jazz).
Karrie Webb	Golf: Winner of the 2000 U.S. Women's Open.
Kathy Baker	Golf: 1985 U.S. Women's Open champion.
Ken Daneyko	Hockey: Winner of the Bill Masterson Trophy in 2000. He played for the New Jersey Devils (Perseverance, Sportsmanship, and Dedication to Hockey Award).
Kickoff	In football, putting the ball into play by kicking it to the opposing team from a stationary position on the ground.
Knuckleball	In baseball, a pitch thrown by gripping the ball with the knuckles of two or three fingers.
KO (Knockout)	In boxing, defeating an opponent by causing him to fall onto the canvas and remain there for a count of ten.
Kurt Warner	Football: NFL Super Bowl MVP in 1999.
Larry Bird	Basketball: High-scoring forward of the Boston Celtics; winner of the NBA Most Valuable Player Award, 1984.
Larry Brown	Football: NFL Super Bowl MVP in 1996.
Laura Davies	Golf: 1987 U.S. Women's Open champion.
Lauri Merten	Golf: Winner of the 1993 U.S. Women's Open.
Layup	In basketball, a shot made by playing the ball off the backboard from close to the basket, usually after driving in.

Lee Janzen	Golf: Won the U.S. Open in 1993 and again in 1998.
Lightweight	In boxing, a BOXER weighing between 127 and 135 pounds.
Lindsay Davenport	Tennis: Won the Women's U.S. Open Championship in 1998 and the Wimbledon Championship in 1999.
Lob	In basketball, volleyball, and tennis, a shot that attains greater height than normal.
Lou Gehrig	Baseball: Hall of Famer; active from 1923 to 1939; one of the all-time greats.
Magic Johnson	Basketball: Winner of the NBA Most Valuable Player Award, 1987; member of the Los Angeles Lakers.
Manny Ramirez	Baseball: Winner of the Hank Aaron Award in 1999.
Marat Safin	Tennis: Won the Men's U.S. Open in 2000.
Marcus Allen	Football: 1981 winner of the Heisman Memorial Trophy (USC).
Mario Andretti	Auto Racing: One of IndyCar's top twenty drivers.
Mario Lemieux	Hockey: Won the Hart Trophy-MVP in 1992, and again in 1996 (Pittsburgh).
Mark Brooks	Golf: Won the U.S. P.G.A. Championship in 1996.
Mark McGwire	Baseball: Broke record for most home runs in a season—162 game season: 70 home runs while playing with the St. Louis Cardinals, NL, 1998, and again in 1999 when he hit 65 home runs.

Mark Messier	Hockey: Won the Hart Trophy-MVP in 1990 (Edmonton), and in 1992 (New York Rangers).
Mark O'Meara	Golf: Won the Masters Tournament in 1996, won the British Open in 1998.
Mark Rypien	Football: NFL Super Bowl MVP in 1992.
Martina Hingis	Tennis: Won the Women's U.S. Open and Wimbledon in 1997.
Martina Navratilova	Tennis: Winner of several indoor, U.S. Open and Wimbledon titles during the late 1970s and 1980s.
Maury Wills	Baseball: Los Angeles Dodgers' shortstop who set a record in 1962 by stealing 104 bases.
Meg Mallon	Golf: Winner of the 1991 U.S. Women's Open.
Michael Andretti	Auto Racing: One of IndyCar's top twenty drivers.
Michael Jordan	Basketball: NBA individual scoring champion 1986 to 1988 and NBA MVP in 1991, 1992, 1996, and 1998 (Chicago Bulls).
Michael Schumacher	Auto Racing: Won the World Grand Prix in 2000.
Michael Spinks	Boxing: World HEAVYWEIGHT champion, 1985 to 1986.
Mickey Mantle	Baseball: New York Yankees outfielder who led the American League in home runs four seasons. During his career with the Yankees from 1952 to 1968, his team won eleven pennants and seven World Championships.

Middleweight	In boxing, a BOXER weighing between 148 and 160 pounds.
Mika Hakkinen	Auto Racing: Won the World Grand Prix in 1998 and 1999.
Mike Ditka	Football: Coach of the 1985 Super Bowl Champion Chicago Bears.
Mike Rozier	Football: 1983 winner of the Heisman Memorial Trophy (Nebraska).
Monica Seles	Tennis: Winner of the U.S. Open in 1991 and 1992, and the 1993 and 1996 Australian Open.
Moses Malone	Basketball: NBA leader in free throws.
Muhammad Ali	Boxing: World HEAVYWEIGHT champion, 1964 to 1967; 1974 to 1978; and 1978 to 1979.
Nancy Lopez	Golf: LPGA leading money winner in 1978, 1979, and 1985.
Nerf	A brand of toy.
Net	In tennis and volleyball, the barrier of meshwork cord that divides the playing field; also, in basketball, the cord under the rim on the backboard.
Nick Faldo	Golf: Won the Masters Tournament in 1989, 1990, and again in 1996; also won the British Open in 1990 and 1992.
Nick Price	Golf: Won the U.S. P.G.A. Championship in 1994.
Nike	A brand of sportswear/shoes.
Nolan Ryan	Baseball: Record holder for most number of lifetime strikeouts by a pitcher (broke 5,000 mark in 1989).

O.B.	"Out of bounds": In football and certain other games, the term applies to a ball out of play.
Olin	A brand of snow ski.
Ottis Anderson	Football: NFL Superbowl MVP in 1990.
Pancho Gonzales	Tennis: Player who dominated the pro tour from 1953 to 1962.
Par	In golf, the score standard for each of the holes on a golf course.
Pat Bradley	Golf: 1981 U.S. Women's Open champion.
Patrick Rafter	Tennis: Won the U.S. Open Championship in 1997 and 1998.
Patty Sheehan	Golf: Winner of the 1992 and 1994 U.S. Women's Open.
Paul Lawrie	Golf: Won the British Open in 1999.
Payne Stewart	Golf: Won the U.S. Open in 1991 and again in 1999, won the U.S. P.G.A. in 1989.
Pele	Soccer: Perhaps the most famous soccer player of all time. A Brazilian by birth, he made headlines in the 1960s and 1970s by his performances in the World Cup competition and retired in 1977.
Penalty	A loss of advantage enforced on a player or team for infraction of a rule.
Pete Rose	Baseball: Leader in total number of lifetime hits (4,256); played mostly with the Cincinnati Reds; suspended in 1989 for betting on baseball.

Pete Sampras	Tennis: Won the U.S. Open Championship in 1990, 1993, 1995, 1996, and 2002. Also won the Wimbledon Championship in 1993–1995 and 1997–2000.
Pistol Pete Maravich	Basketball: Holder of two college top Single-Game Scoring records: 1969 (66 points); 1970 (69 points); also leading individual NBA scorer in 1976 to 1977 (2,273 points).
Pitch	In baseball, the term used for the ball when it is thrown by the PITCHER to the BATTER.
Pitcher	In baseball, one who throws the ball to the BATTER.
Pitchout	In baseball, a PITCH deliberately thrown high and outside making it easy for the CATCHER to retrieve.
Polo	A game played by people on horseback, using a wooden mallet to hit a wooden ball.
Popup	In baseball, a ball hit high into the air by the BATTER.
Puck	In ice hockey, the hard rubber disc used in play instead of a ball.
Punt	In football, a kick in which the ball is kicked when dropped from the hands before it touches the ground.
Putter	In golf, the club used to hit the ball into the cup on the green.
Quarterback	In football, the player who receives the ball from the CENTER, calls the signals, and directs the offensive plays of the team.
Randy Matson	Track and field: The Texas A&M shotputter who broke the world record in 1967; he won an Olympic gold medal the following year.

Rashaan Salaam	Football: 1994 winner of the Heisman Memorial Trophy (Colorado).
Ray Lewis	Football: NFL Superbowl MVP in 2000.
Rebound	In basketball, the act of retrieving and recovering the ball after a missed shot.
Recovery	In football, the act of regaining possession of the ball after a fumble.
Red Auerbach	Basketball: Former coach of the Boston Celtics.
Red Grange	Football: Illinois University player in the 1920s; he was known as "The Galloping Ghost."
Reebok	A brand of sportswear/shoes.
Referee (Ref)	The official who enforces the rules in sports games.
Reggie Jackson	Baseball: American League home run champion 1973, 1975, and 1980.
Richard Krajicek	Tennis: Won Wimbledon in 1996.
Rick Mears	Auto Racing: One of IndyCar's top twenty drivers.
Ricky Williams	Football: Winner of the 1998 Heisman Memorial Trophy (Texas).
Rocky Marciano	Boxing: World HEAVYWEIGHT champion, 1952 to 1956.
Roger Maris	Baseball: Former New York Yankees player; hit 61 home runs in 1961.
Ron Dayne	Football: Winner of the 1999 Heisman Memorial Trophy (Wisconsin).

Rookie	All sports: A player in his or her first year.
Rugby	A British game which has similarities to American football, basketball, soccer, and hockey.
Runner	In baseball, the player who attempts to round the bases; also a person who jogs or runs.
Sacrifice	In baseball, a play in which the BATTER is out but a RUNNER advances to another base.
Safety	In football, the grounding of the ball by the offensive team behind its own goal line; a defensive player farthest from the line of SCRIMMAGE.
Sammy Sosa	Baseball: Hit 50 Home Runs in a Season—162 game season Chicago, NL, 2000, one of the first winners of the Hank Aaron Award 1999.
Sandy Koufax	Baseball: Los Angeles Dodgers pitcher who won the Cy Young Award in 1963, 1965, and 1966.
Scrimmage	A team's practice session.
Se Ri Pak	Golf: Winner of the 1998 U.S. Women's Open.
Serena Williams	Tennis: Won the Women's U.S. Open in 1999 and the Women's Wimbledon doubles with her sister, Venus Williams, in 2000.
Sergei Fedorov	Hockey: Won the Hart Trophy-MVP in 1994 (Detroit).
Server	In tennis, volleyball and certain other games, the player who brings the ball into play.

Shaquille O'Neal	Basketball: Orlando Magic star who was the 1995 scoring leader and NBA MVP in 2000 with the Los Angeles Lakers.
Shortstop	In baseball, the position between second and third base.
Shotgun	A gun that fires multiple pellets through a smooth bore.
Skeet	A sport in which clay targets are thrown into the air and fired at from eight different stations.
Sky Hook	In basketball, a hook shot that attains more than usual height.
Slam Dunk	In basketball, the maneuver in which a player forces the ball into the net from above the rim.
Slingshot	A Y-shaped instrument with elastic bands attached; used for propelling objects.
Snap	In football, the handing of the ball to the QUARTERBACK through the legs of the CENTER.
Sonny Liston	Boxing: World HEAVYWEIGHT champion 1962 to 1964.
Spalding	A brand of sporting goods.
Spar	In boxing, going through the motions of boxing.
Spare	In bowling, knocking down all ten pins with two successive rolls of the ball.
Sparky Anderson	Baseball: Manager of the Cinncinati Reds until 1979 at which time he became manager of the Detroit Tigers.

Speedo	Brand of swimwear.
Spoon	Giving the ball an upward movement in certain games.
Stan Musial	Baseball: Player for the St. Louis Cardinals in the 50s and 60s; a Hall of Famer, Musial held National League records for having played more games (3,026) than any other National Leaguer; he also held league records for most runs batted in, most at bats, most runs scored, and most base hits.
Stefan Edberg	Tennis: Won the U.S. Open Championship in 1991 and 1992.
Steffi Graf	Tennis: Winner of several U.S. Open, Indoor and Wimbledon titles during the 1980s and 1990s.
Steve Elkington	Golf: Won the U.S. P.G.A. in 1999.
Steve Young	Football: NFL Superbowl MVP in 1994.
Steve Yzerman	Hockey: Winner of the 2002 Frank Selke Trophy (Top Defensive Forward Award), for his play with the Detroit Red Wings.
Strike	In baseball, a PITCH that the BATTER misses.
Swish	In basketball, a shot that passes through the rim without touching it.
T. D. (Touchdown)	See TOUCHDOWN.
T.K.O.	Boxing: Technical knockout. This occurs when a match is ended because one of the boxers is unable to continue fighting, but has not been knocked down and counted out by the referee.

Tackle	In football, stopping another player by seizing him and bringing him to the ground; the players positioned between the guard and the end.
Ted Williams	Baseball: Hall of Famer; six time American League batting champion from 1939 to 1960.
Terrell Davis	Football: NFL Superbowl MVP in 1997.
Terry Labonte	Auto Racing: Won the Winston Cup Championship in 1996.
Tiger Woods	Golf: Won the Masters Tournament in 1997, U.S. Open in 2000, won the U.S. Amateur 1994–1996, the U.S. P.G.A. in 1999, and the British Open in 2000, among others.
Tim Brown	Football: 1987 winner of the Heisman Memorial Trophy (Notre Dame).
Tim Duncan	Basketball: NBA Rookie of the Year for 1997–1998 season and MVP for 1998 (San Antonio Spurs).
Todd Helton	Baseball: Winner of the Hank Aaron Award in 2000.
Tom Brady	Football: NFL Superbowl MVP in 2001.
Tom Kite	Golf: Won the U.S. Open in 1992.
Tom Landry	Football: Former coach of the Dallas Cowboys.
Tom Lehman	Golf: Won the British Open in 1996.
Tony Dorsett	Football: 1976 Heisman Memorial Trophy winner (Pittsburgh).

Touchback	In football, touching the ball to the ground behind one's own goal line, the ball having been impelled over the goal line by an opponent.
Touchdown	In football, scoring six points.
Trap	In golf, an area filled with sand to serve as a HAZARD.
Troy Aikman	Football: NFL Superbowl MVP in 1992.
Ty Cobb	Baseball: A Detroit Tigers' player in the early 1900s who had a lifetime batting average of .367 and 4,191 base hits. He was the first member of the National Baseball Hall of Fame.
Ty Detmer	Football: 1990 winner of the Heisman Memorial Trophy (Brigham Young University).
Umpire (Ump)	A person designated to rule on various plays, especially in baseball.
Venus Williams	Tennis: Won the Women's U.S. Open in 2000, the Women's Wimbledon Championship in 2000 and the Women's Wimbledon Doubles with her sister, Serena, in 2000.
Vijay Singh	Golf: Won the Masters Tournament in 2000, won the U.S. P.G.A. Championship in 1998.
Vince Lombardi	Football: Hall of Famer; coach of the Green Bay Packers and Washington Redskins from 1959 to 1970.
Vinny Testaverde	Football: 1986 winner of the Heisman Memorial Trophy (Miami).
Volley	In tennis and volleyball, a series of successive returns of the ball from one side to the other.

Walter Payton	Football: Former all-time NFL leader in rushing yards.
Wayne Grady	Golf: Won the U.S. P.G.A. Championship in 1990.
Wedge	In golf, a club with the head positioned at a large angle to allow for loft when the ball is hit.
Welterweight	In boxing, a BOXER who weighs between 136 and 147 pounds.
Whitey Ford	Baseball: New York Yankees pitcher in the 50s and 60s; holder of the following lifetime World Series records: Most Victories (pitcher), Most Innings Pitched, Most Consecutive Scoreless Innings, and Most Strikeouts by Pitcher.
Willie Mays	Baseball: San Francisco Giants and New York Mets outfielder who had a career batting average of .302. His lifetime total of 660 homers was topped only by BABE RUTH and HANK AARON; Hall of Famer.
Wilson	Brand of sports equipment.
Wilt Chamberlain	Basketball: Star of the Philadelphia Warriors and the Los Angeles Lakers, scoring a record 100 points in one game. He averaged 50.4 points per game during the 1961–1962 season.
Yogi Berra	Baseball: Hall of Famer; active 1946 to 1965. Holder of record number of hits (71) in World Series (lifetime).

"Edsel"

CHAPTER 17

Transportation

. . . He gives you a wave of his long brown tail
Which says: "I'll see you again!"
You'll meet without fail on the Midnight Mail
The Cat of the Railway Train.

T. S. Eliot
from *Old Possum's Book of Practical Cats*

Attention ladies and gentlemen, Flight 524 is now boarding at Gate 3. If you need assistance, please ask your flight attendant for suggestions.

Should you be traveling by car, watch for "Alfa Romeo" and "Ferrari"—they're fast and sometimes difficult to see.

Guarantee your reservation by selecting one of the choices in this chapter. (Cancellations must be made prior to 6 P.M. the day of your pet's arrival.)

Accord — An automobile made by Honda.

Acura — A luxury automobile made by Honda.

Alfa Romeo — An Italian sports car.

Altima — A mid-sized NISSAN sedan.

Amtrak — American Travel Track; railroad with the most extensive passenger service in the United States; created in 1970.

Audi — German-made automobile.

B-52 — A bomber formerly made by BOEING for the U.S. Air Force, extensively used in aerial bombing.

Bentley — A luxury automobile made by ROLLS ROYCE.

Blazer — A recreational vehicle made by Chevrolet.

BMW (Beemer) — A German-made luxury automobile.

Boeing — An aircraft manufacturer.

Boxcar — A fully enclosed freight car.

Bronco — A recreational vehicle made by FORD.

Bugatti — An Italian sports car.

Buggy — A light, horse-drawn carriage.

Buick	An automobile made by General Motors.
Bus	A large passenger vehicle; also sometimes applied to an old car.
Cadillac	A luxury automobile made by General Motors.
Celica	A sports car made by TOYOTA.
Chevy	Chevrolet: an automobile made by General Motors.
Chrysler	An American automobile/manufacturer.
Corvette	A sports car made by Chevrolet. (See CHEVY.)
DeLorean	An automobile designed and manufactured by John DeLorean in the early 1980s in Belfast, Northern Ireland.
DeSoto	An automobile formerly made by CHRYSLER.
Diesel	Type of internal combustion engine, named for a German engineer.
Dodge	An automobile made by CHRYSLER.
Eclipse	A popular MITSUBISHI sports car.
Edsel	An automobile formerly made by FORD.
El Camino	The half-car, half-truck hybrid created by CHEVROLET.
Enola Gay	The name of the bomber used to deploy the first atomic bomb on Hiroshima, Japan.

Escalade	A luxurious S.U.V. manufactured by CADILLAC.
Ferrari	An Italian sports car.
Ford	An American automobile/manufacturer.
Harley	An American-made motocycle manufactured by Harley-Davidson, Inc.
Helicopter (Chopper)	An aircraft powered by a rotor.
Honda	A Japanese automobile/manufacturer.
Hovercraft	A personal transportation device consisting of a flying skateboard from the film *Back to the Future*.
Hummer	The popular S.U.V. manufactured by GMC.
Jaguar	A British luxury automobile.
Jalopy	Run-down or outdated vehicle (usually a car).
Jeep	An American "general purpose vehicle."
Jet	A type of aircraft engine that propels an aircraft forward by expelling exhaust gases rearward.
Jetta	The VOLKSWAGEN sports coupe.
Lamborghini	Expensive Italian automobile.
Lexus	Japanese automobile.

Limo	Short for "limousine."
Lincoln	American automobile made by FORD.
Lotus	British automobile; no longer manufactured.
Mack	The sturdy, chrome-plated bulldog that stands atop the hood of all Mack trucks.
Mazda	A Japanese automobile/manufacturer.
Mercedes	A German luxury automobile manufactured by Mercedes Benz.
MG	A British sports car.
Microbus	The rectangular van popularized by VOLKSWAGEN.
Mitsubishi	A Japanese automobile/manufacturer.
Nissan	A Japanese automobile/manufacturer.
Panzer	A German tank used extensively in World War II.
Peugeot	A French automobile/manufacturer.
Piper	An American aircraft.
Polaris	An American manufacturer of off-road vehicles.
Porsche	A German sports car.
Prelude	An automobile made by HONDA.

Rambler	An automobile manufactured in the United States; it is no longer in production.
Regal	An automobile made by BUICK.
Rickshaw	A light carriage usually pulled by a bicycle or a person.
Rolls Royce	A British luxury automobile/manufacturer.
S.U.V.	The acronym for "Sport Utility Vehicle."
Saturn	Four-cylinder Pontiac automobile.
Schooner	A sailing vessel with two or more masts.
Segway	A personal transportation device invented by Dean Kamen.
Seville	A luxury automobile made by CADILLAC.
Steamer	An early, steam-powered automobile.
Sterling	A British automobile/manufacturer.
Subaru	A Japanese automobile/manufacturer.
Suzuki	A Japanese automobile/manufacturer.
T-Bird	Thunderbird: automobile made by FORD.
Toyota	A Japanese automobile/manufacturer.
Triumph	A British sports car.

Viper	A sports car made by DODGE.
Volkswagen	A German automobile/manufacturer.
Volvo	Swedish automobile.
Yamaha	A Japanese motorcycle/manufacturer.

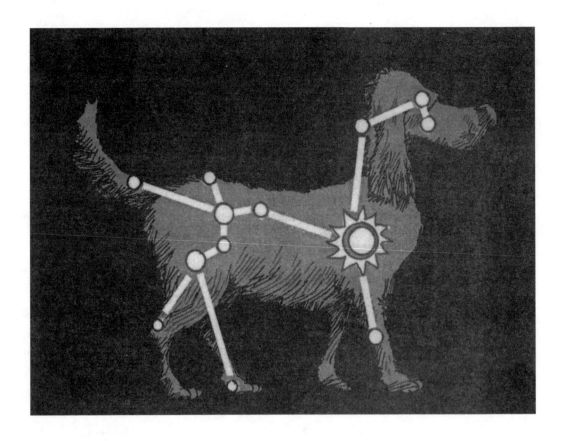

CHAPTER 18

Nature and Science

Nature gives to every time and season some beauties of its own; and from morning to night, as from cradle to the grave, is but a succession of changes so gentle and easy that we can scarcely mark their progress.

Charles Dickens

Take a look at the world of possibilities here. You very well may have a "Gamma" or a "Tiger Lily" just waiting to have the proper title bestowed upon him or her.

Nature and Science

A. C.
Acacia
Acorn
Agate
Alfalfa
Amino
Android
Anion
Anode
Ape
Apollo
Argon
Ariel
Ash
Ashes
Aspen
Aster
Asteroid
Astro
Aurora
Autumn
Avalanche
Axis
Azalea
Badger
Bear

Beaver
Beetle
Begonia
Bengal
Beta
Blizzard
Blossom
Bluebonnet
Boa
Bobcat
Buck
Buckeye
Buckwheat
Buffalo
Bull
Bunny
Buttercup
Butterfly
Byte
Cactus
Calf
Canis Major
Caracal
Carnation
Cat
Catfish

Cathode
Cation
Cheetah
Chick
Cloud
Cobra
Columbine
Comet
Coot
Coral
Corona
Cosmos
Cotton
Coyote
Crab
Cricket
Cub
Cyclone
Cypress
D. C.
Daffodil
Daisy
Dandelion
Delta
Diamond
Dog

Dove
Dynamite
Eagle
Earth
Echo
Eclipse
Equinox
Evening
Feather
Felis
Fern
Fish
Fission
Flint
Flower
Fox
Foxfire
Foxtail
Foxy
Frog
Fungus
Galaxy
Gamma
Garden
'Gator
Goat

Goose	Lava	Mule	Primrose
Grizzly	Leech	Nebula	Puma
Halley's Comet	Leopard	Neon	R.E.M.
Halo	Lightning	Neptune	Rabbit
Hawk	Lilac	Newt	Radar
Hog	Lily	Nocturne	Radon
Holly	Lion	Nova	Rainbow
Honey Bee	Lizard	Nugget	Rose
Honeysuckle	Llama	Nuke	Rosebud
Hormone	Lotus	Ocelot	Ruby
Horse	Lunar	Oleander	Sage
Ice	Lynx	Onyx	Sagebrush
Iguana	Magneto	Orbit	Sassafras
Iris	Magnolia	Orchid	Saturn
Ivy	Marigold	Ozone	Seismis
Jade	Mars	Panda	Serval
Jaguar	Meerkat	Pansy	Shark
Jaguarundi	Megabyte	Panther	Sierra
Jasmine	Mercury	Parasite	Sigma
June Bug	Micro	Petunia	Silk
Jupiter	Micron	Pig	Silver
Kaffir	Mink	Pigeon	Skunk
Kingfish	Mirage	Piranha	Sky
Krypton	Monkey	Pluto	Smoke
Larkspur	Moon	Polar	Snake
Laser	Morning Glory	Poppy	Snapdragon

Nature and Science

Solar
Spider
Squirrel
Star
Steroids ("Roids")
Storm
Sun
Sunset
Sunshine
Sunspot

Supernova
Thor (rocket)
Thunder
Tiger
Tiger Lily
Toad
Topaz
Tornado
Tree
Tropical

Tulip
Tumbleweed
Turbo
Turkey
Turtle
Twilight
Uranus
Ursa Minor
Venus
Weasel

Weed
Whale
Wildcat
Willow
Wolf
Worm
X ray
Zebra
Zinnia

"Lizard"

"Donut"

CHAPTER 19

Foods

. . . eat, that thou mayest have strength, when thou goest on thy way.

I *Samuel* 28:22

In every veterinarian's files, you will find many pets named after foods—from "Bagel" and "Biscuit" to "Taffy" and "Truffle." For a perfectly delicious sampling of names, take a look at this chapter of culinary delights.

Foods

Anchovy

Angel Food

Apple

Asparagus

Avocado

Baby Ruth (a brand of candy bar)

Bagel

Banana

Basil

Beef

Berry

Biscuit

Blackberry

Blueberry

Bosco (a brand of chocolate syrup)

Brie (a cheese)

Bromley (a type of apple)

Brownie

Bubble Gum

Butter

Buttercup

Butterfingers (a brand of chocolate candy bar)

Buttermilk

Caramel

Carrot

Cashew

Casserole

Caviar

Chalupa (a type of Mexican food consisting of a flat fried TORTILLA topped with refried beans and cheese)

Cheddar

Cheerio (a brand of breakfast cereal)

Cheeseburger

Cheesecake

Cheeto (a brand of snack chip)

Cherry

Chestnut

Chicken

Chili

Chip(s)

Chiquita (a brand of bananas)

Chocolate

Chocolate Chip

Chung King (a brand of Chinese food)

Cinnamon

Cinnamon Muffin

Clove

Cocoa

Coconut

Coffee

Cookie

Crackerjack

Crackers

Crepe (a thin pancake)

Crisco (a brand of shortening)

Croissant

Crouton

Cupcake

Curry (a mixture of spices used in Indian cooking)

Custard

Divinity (Fudge)

Donut

Dorito (a brand of corn chip)

Egg Roll

Eggplant

Enchilada (a type of Mexican food consisting of a TORTILLA filled with meat or cheese)

Escargot (a French delicacy of snails prepared in butter, parsley, and garlic)

Fajita (a type of Mexican food consisting of strips of barbecued meat, usually beef or chicken served with TORTILLAS)

Frankfurter

French Fry

Frito (a brand of corn chip)

Fruit Loop (a brand of cereal)

Fudge

Garbanzo (a type of plant with an edible seed)

Ginger

Ginger Snap

Ginseng

Gravy

Grits

Guacamole (mashed and seasoned avacado)

Gum Drop

Gummi Bear (a brand of candy)

Häagen Dazs (a brand of ice cream)

Ham

Hershey (a brand of chocolate)

Honey

Hormel (a brand of meat products)

Hot Dog

Hydrox (a brand of cookies)

Jalapeno (a type of hot pepper)

Jambalaya (a Cajun dish)

Java

Jello

Jelly

Jelly Bean

Jerky (a dried beef snack)

Foods

Kibble (a type of dry dog food)

Kiwi

Kuchen (a German coffee cake with a shortbread crust)

Kumquat (a type of citrus fruit)

Lemon

Lemon Drop

Licorice

Lime

Linguini

Lollipop

Macaroni

Mango

Marshmallow

Meatball

Meringue (stiffly beaten egg whites and sugar used as a dessert topping)

Molasses

Monterey Jack (a type of cheese)

Muffin

Mushroom

Mustard

Nacho (a type of Mexican food consisting of a CHIP topped with refried beans, cheese and/or jalapeño peppers)

Noodle

Nutmeg

O. J. (orange juice)

Oatmeal

Olive

Onion

Orange

Oreo (a brand of cookie)

Oscar Mayer (a brand of meat products)

Pancake

Paprika

Peaches

Peanut(s)

Pepper

Pepper Shaker

Peppermint

Perugina (dark brown chocolate)

Phyllo (paper-thin sheets of pastry used in the preparation of Greek desserts and appetizers)

Pickles

Pinto

Pistachio

Pizza

Popsicle

Popcorn

Pork Chop

Foods

Potato

Pretzel

Pringle

Pudding

Pumpernickel

Pumpkin

Quiche

Raisin

Raisin Bran

Raspberry

Relish

Rhubarb

Ribeye

Ritz (a brand of cracker)

Sage

Salt

Sassafras (a type of tea)

Sauce

Sausage

Schnitzel

Sesame

Shortcake

Shrimp

Sirloin

Skippy (a brand of peanut butter)

Smuckers (a brand of jams and jellies)

Snickers (a brand of candy bar)

Souffle

Soup

Spaghetti

Spearmint

Spice

Spicey

Spud (Potato)

Squash

Strawberry

Strudel

Sugar

Sundae

Sushi (a type of Japanese food consisting of raw fish and seasoned rice)

Syrup

T-Bone

Tabasco (a brand of hot sauce)

Taco (a type of Mexican food consisting of a folded TORTILLA filled with meat, cheese and spices)

Taffy

Tamale (a type of Mexican food consisting of minced meat and spices rolled in a corn dough and cooked in the wrapping of a corn husk)

Tangerine

Tapioca Pudding

Tater (potato)

Tenderloin

Tiramisu (an Italian dessert)

Toffee (a hard or chewy candy)

Tofu

Tomato

Tootsie Roll

Tortilla (a type of Mexican food consisting of a thin baked circular piece of dough, the main ingredient being corn or flour)

Truffle

Turnip

Twinkie (a brand of snack cake)

Vichyssoise

Waffle

Weiner

Wheaties (a brand of breakfast cereal)

Wishbone

Ziplock (a brand of food storage bags)

"Brandy"

CHAPTER 20

Liquors and Drinks

*Let your boat of life be light, packed with only what you
need—a homely home and simple pleasures, one or two
friends, worth the name, someone to love you, a cat, a dog,
and a pipe or two, enough to eat and enough to drink; for
thirst is a dangerous thing.*

Jerome Klapka Jerome
from *Three Men in a Boat*

Belly up to the bar.... Undoubtedly, some of the following names
were selected after the pet owners did just that. (Not all the drinks
listed are alcoholic).

Cheers to you and your new pet!

Liquors and Drinks

Amaretto	Almond LIQUEUR.
Amstel	A brand of beer.
Asahi	A brand of Japanese beer.
Asti	Asti Spumante.
Bahama Mama	A cocktail.
Bartles (Bartles and Jaymes)	A brand of wine cooler.
Beaujolais	A type of red wine.
Beaulieu	A California winery.
Beck's	A brand of German beer.
Big Red	A brand of soft drink.
Bordeaux	A type of red wine.
Bourbon	A liquor distilled from a mash of corn, rye, and malted barley.
Brandy	A liquor distilled from fermented grapes or other fruit.
Budweiser	A brand of American beer.
Cabernet (Sauvignon)	A type of red wine.

Canadian Club (C. C.)	A brand of Canadian WHISKEY.
Cappucino	A drink made with strong coffee and hot milk.
Celis	A brand of beer.
Chablis	A type of white wine.
Champagne	An effervescent wine.
Chardonnay	A type of white wine.
Chianti	An Italian red wine.
Chivas (Regal)	A brand of Scotch WHISKEY.
Claret	A type of red wine.
Coca-Cola (Coke)	A brand of soft drink.
Cocoa	A beverage made from the defatted portion of the cocoa bean.
Coffee	A beverage made from roasted and ground coffee beans.
Cognac	A type of French BRANDY.
Coors	An American beer.
Corona	A brand of Mexican beer.
Courvoisier	A brand of French COGNAC.

Liquors and Drinks

Cuervo	A brand of Mexican TEQUILA.
Daiquiri	A frozen or iced drink made with fruit juice, sugar, and rum.
Dewars	A brand of Scotch WHISKEY.
Dixie	A brand of American beer.
Dos Equis	A brand of Mexican beer.
Dr. Pepper	A brand of soft drink.
Foster's	A brand of beer.
Gin	A liquor flavored with juniper berries.
Glen Ellen	A brand of wine.
Grolsch	A brand of Dutch beer.
Harvey Wallbanger	A cocktail.
Heineken	A brand of Dutch beer.
Hurricane	A cocktail.
Jack Daniels	A brand of Tennesee WHISKEY.
Jax	A brand of American beer.
Jaymes (Bartles and Jaymes)	A brand of wine cooler.

Jigger(s)	A measure used in making mixed drinks (usually 1½ ounces).
Kahlúa	A brand of Mexican coffee liqueur.
Kamikaze	A cocktail.
Killian('s)	A brand of American beer.
Kirin	A brand of Japanese beer.
Lemonade	A beverage made with lemon juice, sugar, and water.
Liqueur	A sweetened, flavored liquor.
Mai Tai	A cocktail.
Margarita	A cocktail.
Martini	A cocktail.
Merlot	A type of red wine.
Miller	A brand of American beer.
Mint Julep	A cocktail.
Mocha	A rich Arabian coffee; a drink made by mixing coffee with chocolate.
Molson	A brand of Canadian beer.
Moosehead	A brand of Canadian beer.

Liquors and Drinks

Moretti	A brand of Italian beer.
Mr. Pibb	A brand of soft drink.
Napa	A valley in California where grapes are grown to make wine.
Nehi	A brand of soft drink.
Old Milwaukee	A brand of American beer.
Pabst (Blue Ribbon)	A brand of American beer.
Pacifico	A brand of beer.
Pearl	A brand of Texas beer.
Pepe Lopez	A brand of Mexican TEQUILA.
Pepsi	A brand of soft drink.
Peroni	A brand of Italian beer.
R. C. Cola	A brand of soft drink.
Red Dog	A brand of beer.
Red Stripe	A brand of beer.
Root Beer	A soft drink.
Sake	A Japanese alcoholic beverage made from rice.

Samuel Adams	A brand of American beer.
Samuel Smith('s)	A brand of British beer.
Sapporo	A brand of Japanese beer.
Schnapps	Various flavored LIQUEURS.
Scotch	A WHISKEY distilled from malted barley.
Seagram's	A brand of American blended WHISKEY.
Sebastiani	A California wine/winery.
Seven Up	A brand of soft drink.
Shasta	A brand of soft drink.
Shiner Bock	A brand of beer.
Singapore Sling	A cocktail.
Slice	A brand of soft drink.
Soda	A flavored soft drink; unflavored carbonated water; a mixture of the latter with ice cream and syrup.
Soda Pop	A flavored soft drink.
Spatlese	A type of German white wine.
Sprite	A brand of soft drink.

267

Liquors and Drinks

Spritzer · A cocktail.

St. Pauli Girl · A brand of German beer.

Starbucks · A brand of coffee.

Stolychnaya (Stoli) · A brand of Russian VODKA.

Stroh's · A brand of American beer.

"Schnapps"

Superior	A brand of Mexican beer.
Swizzle	A cocktail.
Tea	A beverage brewed from the leaves of the tea plant.
Tecate	A brand of Mexican beer.
Tequila	A liquor distilled from mescal.
Tonic	Anything that refreshes or rejuvenates; a regional carbonated water.
Tucher Weiss	A brand of beer.
Two Fingers	A brand of Mexican TEQUILA.
Verdillac	A French wine.
Vodka	A colorless, "neutral" liquor distilled from grain.
Watney's	A brand of British beer.
Whiskey	Any liquor distilled from a grain mash.
Wild Turkey	A brand of Kentucky WHISKEY.
Xing Tao	A brand of Chinese beer.
Zima	A brand of American beer.
Zinfandel	A red, white, or blush wine made from California's Zinfandel grape.

"L.L. Bean"

CHAPTER 21

Fashion and Cosmetics

The world is governed more by appearances than by realities, so that it is fully as necessary to seem to know something as to know it.

Daniel Webster

You don't have to be a devotee of design to consider some of the names in this chapter. The right name for your fashionable pet might be close at hand . . . or on your feet!

Aca Joe	A brand of clothing.
Amethyst	A semiprecious stone.
Anaïs Anaïs	A brand of fragrance.
Benetton	A chain of clothing stores.
Blush	A type of cosmetic used to heighten facial color.
Bongo	A brand of clothing.
Bubble Bath	A scented soap used to produce masses of bubbles in bath water.
— Calvin Klein	Designer; brand of clothing.
Cambridge	A brand of clothing.
Carolina Herrera	A brand of fragrance named for the designer.
Cashmere	A fine woolen fabric made from the hair of the kashmir goat.
Chanel	Designer; brand of clothing and fragrance.
Chaps	Protective leather leg coverings worn by cowboys. Also a brand of cologne.
Chic	A brand of clothing; highly fashionable.
Chloë	A brand of fragrance.
Christian Dior	Designer; brand of clothing; fragrance and cosmetics.

Claiborne (Liz)	Designer; brand of clothing and fragrance.
Confetti	A brand of clothing.
— Cover Girl	A brand of cosmetics.
Diamond	A precious stone.
Drakkar	A brand of cologne.
Elle	A fashion magazine.
Emerald	A precious stone.
Esprit	A brand of clothing.
Finesse	A brand of shampoo/hair products.
Forenza	A brand of clothing.
Genera	A brand of clothing.
Giorgio	A brand of fragrance.
Girbaud	A brand of clothing.
Gitano	A brand of clothing.
Givenchy	Designer; brand of clothing, fragrance, and cosmetics.
GQ	Men's fashion and lifestyle magazine.

Gucci	Designer; brand of clothing, handbags, etc.
Guess	A brand of clothing.
Haggar	A brand of clothing.
Halston	Designer; brand of cologne and fragrance.
Jack & Jill	A brand of clothing.
Jade	A gemstone, usually pale green or white.
Jasmine	A brand of fragrance.
L. L. Bean	A mail-order clothing company and brand of outdoor clothing products.
Laura Ashley	Designer; brand of clothing, linens, and fragrance.
Lee	A brand of sportswear.
Levi	A brand of sportswear.
Lipstick	A type of cosmetic used to heighten lip color.
Maybelline	A brand of cosmetics.
Obsession	A brand of fragrance and cologne.
Onyx	A black gemstone used in jewelry.
Opal	A gemstone.

Opium	A brand of fragrance and cologne.
Oxford	A style of shoe with laces; a type of cotton cloth.
Paco Rabanne	A brand of fragrance.
Paisley	A multicolored pattern of curving shapes used to decorate fabric.
Paloma Picasso	Designer; daughter of artist Pablo Picasso.
Pappagallo	A brand of shoes.
Pairs	A brand of fragrance.
Passion	A brand of fragrance.
Pearl	A lustrous concretion formed inside an oyster.
Poison	A brand of fragrance.
Polo	A brand of clothing designed by RALPH LAUREN.
Poncho	(1) A loose fitting piece of clothing worn by some Mexicans. (2) A garment made of plastic or other waterproof material, used as a raincoat.
Powder Puff	A fluffy applicator for face or body powder.
Ralph Lauren	Designer; brand of clothing.
Revlon	A brand of cosmetics.
Rolex	A brand of wristwatch.

Fashion and Cosmetics

Ruby	A precious stone.
Sapphire	A precious stone.
Satin	A lustrous fabric made of silk or rayon.
Seiko	A brand of wristwatch from Japan.
Shalimar	A brand of fragrance.
Soapy	Sudsy.
Spats	Shoe coverings.
Spiegel	A mail-order clothing company.
Sterling	Silver that is nearly pure (925 parts silver to 75 parts copper).
Tiara	A crown of jewels.
Tiffany	A fashionable jewelry store in New York City.
Topaz	A semi-precious stone.
Tux	Short for tuxedo—formal attire for a man.
Vanderbilt (Gloria)	Designer; brand of clothing and fragrance.
Velvet	A fabric made of silk, rayon, etc., which has a soft, luxuriant texture.
Vidal Sassoon	Designer; brand of clothing and hair-care products.

Wrangler	A brand of clothing.
Ysatis	A brand of perfume.
Yves Saint Laurent	Designer; brand of clothing.

"Moritz" and *"Max"*

CHAPTER 22

Pairs

. . . people . . . name (their) dogs
 Pitter and Patter,
 Willy and Nilly,
 Helter and Skelter,
 Namby and Pamby,
 Hugger and Mugger, and even
 Wishy and Washy,
 Ups and Daisy,
 Fitz and Startz,
 Fetch and Carrie, and
 Pro and Connie.

James Thurber
from *How to Name a Dog*

So you're having twice as much fun now that you have two little critters, right? Well, relax and enjoy it by taking a look at these interesting combinations. Perhaps you'll find that very special one-of-a-kind name for your very special two-of-a-kind friends.

Pairs

Abbott & Costello (See Chapter 11)

Adam & Eve (See Chapter 7)

Amos & Andy (See Chapter 11)

Anion & Cation (See Chapter 18)

Anode & Cathode (See Chapter 18)

Antony & Cleopatra

Apples & Oranges

Aurora & Boring Alice (See Chapter 10)

Back & Forth

Barney & Fred (See Chapter 14)

Barnum & Bailey (See Chapter 5)

Baron & Baroness

Bartles & Jaymes (See Chapter 20)

Baucis & Philemon (See Chapter 6)

Bert & Ernie (See Chapter 11)

Betty & Wilma (See Chapter 14)

Big & Bad

Biton & Cleobis (See Chapter 6)

Black & White

Bogey & Bacall (See Chapter 11)

Bonnie & Clyde

Briggs & Stratton (a type of engine)

Cagney & Lacey

Cain & Abel (See Chapter 7)

Calvin & Hobbes (See Chapter 14)

Carlos & Charlie (a restaurant in Mexico)

Castor & Pollux (See Chapter 6)

Chainsaw & Sawdust

Cheech & Chong (comedians)

Chips & Salsa

Count & Countess

Cupid & Psyche (See Chapter 6)

Czar & Czarina

David & Goliath (See Chapter 7)

Ding & Ling

Dagwood & Blondie (See Chapter 14)

Down & Out

Dr. Jekyll & Mr. Hyde

Dude & Dudette

Duke & Duchess

East & West

Elvis & Priscilla

Emperor & Empress

Felix & Oscar (See Chapter 11)

Ferdinand & Isabella (See Chapter 5)

First & Ten

Foot Loose & Fancy Free

Frank and Stein

Fred & Ethel (See Chapter 11)

George & Gracie (See Chapter 11)

Get Off the Rug & You Too

Glimmer & Twynkle

Goodness & Mercy

Groucho & Harpo (See Chapter 15)

Happy & Sad

Harley & Davidson

Hera & Zeus (See Chapter 6)

Hero & Leander (See Chapter 6)

Him & Her (See Chapter 5)

Hollywood & Vine

Hoot & Holler

Hunkie & Dorie

Hunnies & Funnies

Itsy & Bitsy

Pairs

King & Queen

Kit & Kaboodle

Kut & Kutta (See Chapter 9)

Lady & Tramp (See Chapter 11)

Laurel & Hardy (See Chapter 11)

Laverne & Shirley (See Chapter 11)

Licker & Whiner

Lord & Lady

Love 'Em & Leave 'Em

Lucy & Ricky (See Chapter 11)

Marco & Polo

Mason & Dixon

Max & Moritz (See Chapter 10)

Mickey & Minnie (See Chapter 14)

Mutt & Jeff (See Chapter 14)

Napoleon & Josephine (See Chapter 5)

Nieman & Marcus (See Chapter 12)

Nip & Tuck

North & South

Now & Then

Null & Void

Orpheus & Eurydice (See Chapter 6)

Ozzie & Harriet (See Chapter 11)

Patience & Fortitude (See Chapter 10)

Patriarch & Matriarch

Pete & Repeat

Ping & Pong

Porgy & Bess

Prince & Princess

Prose & Kahn

Pyramus & Thisbe (See Chapter 6)

Ralph & Alice (See Chapter 11)

Regis & Kathie Lee

Ren & Stimpy (See Chapter 14)

Romeo & Juliet (See Chapter 10)

Rough & Ready

Ruff & Tuff

Salt & Pepper

Samson & Delilah (See Chapter 7)

Scarlett & Rhett (See Chapter 11)

Simon & Garfunkel

Simon & Schuster (See Chapter 10)

Sonny & Cher (See Chapter 15)

Stanley & Livingstone (See Chapter 5)

Starsky & Hutch (characters in T.V. series)

Sugar & Spice

Taco & Chalada (See Chapter 19)

Teeter & Totter

Thunder & Lightning

Tick & Tock

Tom & Jerry (See Chapter 14)

Topsy & Turvy

Venus & Adonis (See Chapter 10)

Waylon & Willy

When & If

Wilbur & Charlotte (See Chapter 10)

Wilbur & Orville (See Chapter 5)

Woofer & Tweeter (See Chapter 15)

"Good, Bad & Ugly"

CHAPTER 23

Trios

> *Love the earth and sun and the animals, despise riches, . . .*
> *have patience and indulgence toward the people, . . . dismiss*
> *whatever insults your soul, and your very flesh shall be a*
> *great poem.*

> Walt Whitman

Here's a sampling of the endless possibilities for owners of three pets.

For additional ideas, consider the topics and names in Chapters 1–21; staying within a given category for all three names makes a more interesting combination.

One word of caution: Names that rhyme may sound confusing to animals. However, if they already seem confused, try Moe, Larry, and Curly.

Trios

Blood, Sweat & Tears (See Chapter 15)

Flopsy, Mopsy & Cottontail (See Chapter 10)

Good, Bad & Ugly

Hey You, Who Me & Yeah You

Hickory, Dickory & Dock

Huey, Dewey & Louie (See Chapter 14)

Kukla, Fran & Ollie (See Chapter 11)

Larry, Moe & Curly (See Chapter 11)

Peter, Paul & Mary

Upstairs, Downstairs & Mezzanine

REGISTERING A NAME WITH THE AMERICAN KENNEL CLUB

If your dog will be registered by the American Kennel Club (AKC), you need to follow the guidelines established by the AKC:

The person who owns the dog and applies to register it has the right to name the dog. On registration applications issued starting in mid-1989 a space is provided for only one name choice. Registration applications issued prior to that time have spaces for two name choices. It is not necessary to indicate a second name choice, but if you do, consider both names carefully. There is always a chance that the second will be approved and, therefore, it should be equally desirable by the owner. A dog's name may not be changed after it is registered.

Name choices are limited to 25 letters.

No Arabic or Roman numerals may be included in name choices, and no written number is permitted at the end of names. AKC reserves the right to assign a Roman numeral. AKC permits thirty-seven dogs of each breed to be assigned the same name, and many common names such as Spot, Snoopy, Lassie, King, etc., are fully allotted. The shorter the name choice the greater the chances that AKC will assign a Roman numeral or that the name may not be accepted at all. The longer and more unique the name chosen, the greater the chance for approval. The easiest way to lengthen a name is to incorporate your surname, for example, "Smith's Spot" instead of Spot.

Remember that the dog's "call name," that is, the name he responds to, does not have to be the same as his registered name. If you name your dog "Spot" and it is not approved, you may continue to call him "Spot," even though his registered name may be different.

Incorrect spelling and grammar are not corrected by AKC. Names are approved as submitted. A change in spelling is considered a change of name and is not allowed.

Do not include:

1. Names of prominent people, living or recently deceased.
2. Words or abbreviations that imply AKC titles (Champ, Winner).
3. The words: Dog, Male, Sire, Bitch, Female, Dam, Kennel.
4. Words that are disparaging or obscene.
5. Roman or Arabic numerals.
6. Breed names alone.*

To obtain applications or more information concerning AKC registration and requirements, write to:

American Kennel Club
51 Madison Avenue
New York, New York 10010

*American Kennel Club, *Dogs, General Information* (New York: American Kennel Club), pp. 21–22. Used with permission.

Help me make *The Best Pet Name Book Ever* even better!

Just in case I forgot your favorite pet name, please send it to me so I can include it in the next edition of this book.

If there is a story or explanation behind your choice of name, please include that, too.

Send all nominations for the next edition to:

Wayne Bryant Eldridge
c/o Barron's Educational Series, Inc.
250 Wireless Boulevard
Hauppauge, NY 11788

BARRON'S BOOKS FOR DOG OWNERS

Barron's offers a wonderful variety of books for dog owners and prospective owners, all written by experienced breeders, trainers, veterinarians, or qualified experts on canines. Most books are heavily illustrated with handsome color photos and instructive line art. They'll tell you facts you need to know, and give you advice on purchasing, feeding, grooming, training, and keeping a healthy pet.

Before You Buy That Puppy
ISBN 0-8120-1750-1

Careers With Dogs
ISBN 0-7641-0503-5

Civilizing Your Puppy, 2nd Ed.
ISBN 0-8120-9787-4

Communicating With Your Dog
ISBN 0-7641-0758-5

The Complete Book of Dog Breeding
ISBN 0-8120-9604-5

Doggy Fashion
ISBN 0-7641-2584-2

Encyclopedia of Dog Breeds
ISBN 0-7641-5097-9

Fun and Games With Your Dog
ISBN 0-8120-9721-1

How to Teach Your Old Dog New Tricks
ISBN 0-8120-4544-0

Puppies
ISBN 0-8120-6631-6

Show Me!
ISBN 0-8120-9710-6

Train Your Dog
ISBN 0-7641-0967-7

The Trick is in the Training
ISBN 0-7641-0492-6

Barron's Educational Series, Inc.
250 Wireless Blvd., Hauppauge, NY 11788 • To order toll-free: 1-800-645-3476
In Canada: Georgetown Book Warehouse • 34 Armstrong Ave., Georgetown, Ont. L7G
4R9 Order toll-free in Canada: 1-800-247-7160
Or order from your favorite bookstore or pet store
Visit our web site at: www.barronseduc.com

(#111) R4/03

BARRON'S BOOKS FOR CAT LOVERS

Barron's offers a wide variety of books for cat fanciers, cat owners, and prospective owners looking for more information. All have been written by experienced breeders, veterinarians, or qualified experts on felines—and most are heavily illustrated with handsome color photos and instructive line art. They'll tell you what you need to know about feeding, grooming, training, showing, and keeping a healthy cat.

Communicating with Your Cat
ISBN 0-7641-0855-7

The Complete Book of Cat Breeding
ISBN 0-8120-9764-5

The Complete Book of Cat Care
ISBN 0-8120-4613-7

Encyclopedia of Cat Breeds
ISBN 0-7641-5067-7

Guide to a Well-Behaved Cat
ISBN 0-8120-1476-6

Natural Health Care for Your Cat
ISBN 0-7641-0123-4

Barron's Educational Series, Inc.
250 Wireless Blvd., Hauppauge, NY 11788 • To order toll-free: 1-800-645-3476
In Canada: Georgetown Book Warehouse • 34 Armstrong Ave.,
Georgetown, Ont. L7G 4R9 • Order toll-free in Canada: 1-800-247-7160
Or order from your favorite bookstore or pet store
Visit our web site at: www.barronseduc.com

(#65b) R4/03

"A solid bet for first-time pet owners"
—*Booklist*

We've taken all the best features of our popular Pet Owner's Manuals and added **more** expert advice, **more** sparkling color photographs, **more** fascinating behavioral insights, and fact-filled profiles on the leading breeds. Indispensable references for pet owners, ideal for people who want to compare breeds before choosing a pet. Over 120 illustrations per book – 55 to 60 in full color!

THE AFRICAN GREY PARROT HANDBOOK
THE AMERICAN PIT BULL TERRIER HANDBOOK
THE NEW AUSTRALIAN PARAKEET HANDBOOK
THE BEAGLE HANDBOOK
THE NEW BIRD HANDBOOK
THE BOXER HANDBOOK
THE NEW CANARY HANDBOOK
THE CAT HANDBOOK
THE CHAMELEON HANDBOOK
THE CHIHUAHUA HANDBOOK
THE COCKATIEL HANDBOOK
THE DOG HANDBOOK
THE NEW DUCK HANDBOOK
THE FERRET HANDBOOK
THE FINCH HANDBOOK
THE GERMAN SHEPHERD HANDBOOK
THE NEW GOAT HANDBOOK
THE GOLDEN RETRIEVER HANDBOOK
THE GUINEA PIG HANDBOOK
THE HAMSTER HANDBOOK
THE IGUANA HANDBOOK
THE JACK RUSSELL TERRIER HANDBOOK
THE LABRADOR RETRIEVER HANDBOOK
THE LOVEBIRD HANDBOOK
THE NATURAL AQUARIUM HANDBOOK
THE PARAKEET HANDBOOK
THE PARROTLET HANDBOOK
THE NEW PARROT HANDBOOK
THE RABBIT HANDBOOK
THE ROTTWEILER HANDBOOK
THE SALTWATER AQUARIUM HANDBOOK
THE SPORTING SPANIEL HANDBOOK
THE NEW TERRIER HANDBOOK
THE YORKSHIRE TERRIER HANDBOOK

"*Stunning*"
–Roger Caras
Pets & Wildlife

Books may be purchased at your local bookstore, pet shop, or by mail from Barron's. Enclose check or money order for the total amount plus sales tax where applicable and 18% for postage and handling (minimum charge $5.95). Prices subject to change without notice.

Barron's Educational Series, Inc.
250 Wireless Blvd., Hauppauge, NY 11788
In Canada: Georgetown Book Warehouse
34 Armstrong Ave., Georgetown, Ont. L7G 4R9

(#63) R 4/03

BARRON'S PET REFERENCE BOOKS